Planning for the 21st Century

A Guide for Community Colleges

William A. Wojciechowski, Ed.D.
and
Dedra Manes

ISBN: 1-58597-205-3

Library of Congress Control Number: 2003113156

A division of Squire Publishers, Inc.
4500 College Blvd.
Leawood, KS 66211
1/888/888-7696
www.leatherspublishing.com

TABLE OF CONTENTS

EXHIBITS *(Continued)*

ACKNOWLEDGEMENTS

I would like to thank my husband, Rob, for his encouragement and time spent editing and helping with the technological aspects of this project; my daughters, Aubrey and Lauren for their patience and providing the motivation to achieve one of my life goals in writing this book; my friends and family for their constant and loving support; and Dr. William Wojciechowski, who has patiently mentored and challenged me not only in the field of higher education, but in life for the past 15 years. None of my life efforts would be possible without the grace and goodness of my Heavenly Father who has promised me that "I can do all things through Him who strengthens me" (Phil. 4:13).

— Dedra Manes

All through my personal and professional life my wife, Terri, has encouraged me to seek my goals even at the expense of her own. I wish, here, to acknowledge her encouragement and sacrifice and to thank her for her inspiration. When I first mentioned writing this manuscript, her first words were, "Go for it!" I also wish to thank Elizabeth Bible, my administrative assistant for the last 15 years, for her assistance in preparing numerous drafts and formats of the exhibits. Finally, I want to acknowledge the contributions of my colleague, Dedra Manes, who over the years helped develop and refine one of the most dependable and sound planning processes to arrive on the college scene in the last 20 years.

—William A. Wojciechowski, Ed.D.
President, Pratt Community College

PREFACE

Planning for the 21st Century — A Guide for Community Colleges is a powerful tool. It presents all the elements for the development of a series of successful *futures*. The material presented is straightforward and concise, making it an ideal "manual" for every member of the planning team, assuring that all are following the same map, to the same place.

One aspect, however, sets it apart from other planning guides, and that is acknowledging the importance of governance in the process. Identifying the critical role of the board of trustees in connecting with the community for input and feedback, their role setting budget parameters, advocating for resources, monitoring and assessing the results will prove to be the key ingredient in this guide's success.

Introduction. Here the authors provide us with a context and rationale for their approach with an overview of the various traditional approaches to the planning process. Long range, strategic and tactical planning methods are all compared to the author's preferred mid-range process.

Chapter 1: Where It Begins ... developing a mission, purpose and vision for your college. In this chapter the authors explore the critical role of mission, purpose and vision in the planning process. We are carefully guided through each step necessary to establish a current mission statement clarified by distinct institutional purposes and focused on a common vision of the institution's service to the community.

Chapter 2: What It Takes ... effectively engaging the board of trustees in the mid-range planning process. Taking a bold and important step, we are encouraged to actively engage the board in the mid-range planning process. Strategies to develop the board's understanding of the process and their role in assuring its success are discussed. Key elements include the board's review of community input in the context of the current social, political and economic environment is presented. The board's continuous involvement in assuring the success of the planning effort and the need for board continuing education is stressed.

Chapter 3: What We Know ... the environmental scan and how to use it effectively for mid-range planning. Using external and internal data sources essential to establishing institutional goals are explored in depth. We are provided with suggestions for the use of community forums and various survey techniques in developing the information necessary for informed goal setting.

Chapter 4: Where We Should Go ... practicing mid-range planning. Here we are provided with an overview of the entire planning cycle. We begin with a process for developing effective goals and objectives based on analyses of environmental scanning data, followed by the establishment of a monitoring process and a description of the written planning document. Here again the board of trustees plays a crucial role in the authors' approach. The board is engaged in a workshop prior to their adoption of the budget and receives staff-generated reports to complete the planning cycle.

Chapter 5: What Makes It Work ... linking planning to the budgeting, facilities and assessment elements. Here we are provided with an important in-depth look at how the structure of the mid-range plan is used to support the connection between planning and the budgeting, facilities and assessment processes. The importance of this connection or "linkage" is described as essential to our success.

Chapter 6: Keep It Going ... ensuring that the mid-range planning process is here to stay. In this chapter we are encouraged to undertake activities such as the ongoing reporting of the status of goal attainment to assure that the staff, community and board of trustees remain engaged in the process.

This clear, crisp approach to a process often made too complex to be practical concludes with a series of exhibits to get us started down the road to our next, our continuing successful community college future.

— *Ray Taylor*
Executive Director
Association of Community College Trustees

INTRODUCING THE PLANNING FUNCTION IN COMMUNITY COLLEGES

- Planning both a governance and administrative function
- Definition of planning
- Types of planning – a comparative analysis
- Guidelines for choosing a planning model

Planning – A Governance and Administrative Function

Community colleges are full-fledged members of the public, non-profit corporate sector of American business and industry. Like other corporate members, community colleges have their own necessary but sometimes unwanted bureaucratic structure, i.e., a charted organization with a clearly defined chain of command, and functions which include: planning, organizing, staffing, directing, coordinating, reporting and budgeting. Most modern management texts list these functions in one form or another, sometimes combining two or three under a single heading, but generally beginning with planning as the first step of the management process. Oddly enough, in the process of governing, which is clearly the responsibility of an appointed or elected board of trustees at the state, regional or local level, planning is also considered a primary function of governance. It is for this reason that the planning which the board does to formulate policy is often confused with the planning that a college administration does prior to taking action to implement that policy. This source of confusion, which often is not recognized and addressed, can lead to strained working relationships between the governing board and its administration. Planning for policy and planning for action, though they may share the same process, produce very different outcomes. The latter is more specific because it details responsibilities in terms of action offices, target dates and projected outcomes. The projected outcomes are the implementation and the outgrowth of governing board policies.

Definition of Planning

Planning, for the most part, is a decision making process which incorporates a host of variables in a defined environment leading to effective, economical future outcomes. In effect, planning is the first step in guiding change in a positive, purposeful way. Beginning with the most basic of definitions[1], planning is a proposed goal accompanied by a detailed program of events worked out beforehand leading to the accomplishment of that goal. Planning is systematic and it doesn't occur in isolation or while being insulated from the environment. George Steiner, a successful corporate consultant whose work helped lay the foundation for several theoretical approaches to planning – management by objectives, PERT diagrams, Planned Programs Budgeting Systems (PPBS) and others — defined planning in one of the most comprehensive and thought provoking books on goal directed planning in this manner:

> Planning is a process that begins with objectives; defines strategies, policies, and detailed plans to achieve them; which establishes an organization to implement decisions; and includes a review of performance and feedback to introduce a new planning cycle.[2]

In his continued discussion on planning, Steiner emphasizes that, in this mode, plans should be formally prepared and written into a published document. Furthermore, the planning document should be "to the fullest extent objective, factual, logical and realistic."[3]

Types of Planning – A Comparative Analysis

To plan is to deal with future uncertainty, in an informed manner, in order to minimize risk to the organization. The farther into the future that an organization plans, the greater the risk it faces as the uncertainty grows. However, regardless of the risk and the uncertainty, an institution must have a vision of its future at whatever point it chooses to park, or the institution will jeopardize its opportunities to grow and to prosper. Planning occurs across a full spectrum of an institution's continuum – from planning for the present (operational) to planning for the next decade and beyond (strategic). Exhibit I-1 on the next page provides an excellent illustration of the planning continuum while identifying the various types of planning that exist along that continuum.[4] The reader will note that bracketed between the three to five year points on the time horizon is [MID-RANGE] planning which is fast becoming the planning model of choice among business, industrial and non-

EXHIBIT I-1

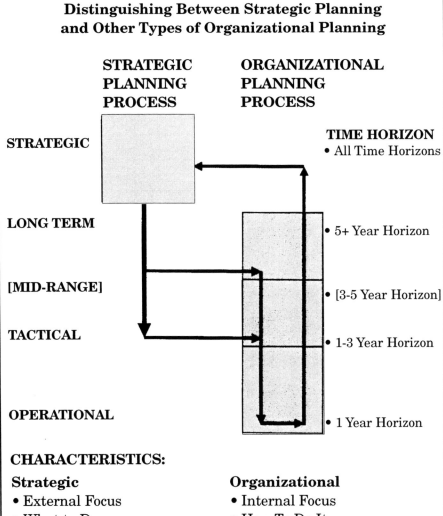

**Distinguishing Between Strategic Planning
and Other Types of Organizational Planning**

STRATEGIC
PLANNING
PROCESS

ORGANIZATIONAL
PLANNING
PROCESS

STRATEGIC

TIME HORIZON
• All Time Horizons

LONG TERM

• 5+ Year Horizon

[MID-RANGE]

• [3-5 Year Horizon]

TACTICAL

• 1-3 Year Horizon

OPERATIONAL

• 1 Year Horizon

CHARACTERISTICS:

Strategic
• External Focus
• What to Do
• Macro Issues
• Boundary Spanning
• Continual Scanning Process
  to Notice Changes Occurring
  Irregularly, Dictated by
  Environment
• Expert Participation

Organizational
• Internal Focus
• How To Do It
• Impact of Macro Issues on
  Micro Issues
• Tied to Organizational Units
• Regular Processes Dictated by
  Organizational Cycles
• Linked to Budget/Resource
  Allocation Process
• Constituent Participation

profit institutions in this fast paced, high technology environment.[5] A walk through the various types of planning along the continuum provides a better understanding of different planning processes that occur in an organization, the advantages associated with each and a comparative analysis between these and the mid-range planning process which the authors advocate and prefer.

Operational planning focuses on the criticality of dealing with immediate issues, resolving them permanently, or buying time to affect permanent solutions. Norris and Poulton best define operational planning in this manner:

> In some applications, operational planning is called problem-focused, contingency, or performance-improvement planning. **Problem-focused or contingency planning** is generally short term and highly focused, dealing with problems that exist today. The solutions to these problems may be achievable in the long term, but the activities are targeted to deal with current problems ... to tune and improve performance of current operations ... (and) viewing operational planning as a practical, immediate, short-term activity having concrete results.[6]

Generally, an institution's administration employs operational planning to make modifications and minor adjustments to correct deviations from established objectives in order to bring more control to achieving planned outcomes. A common example of operational planning follows in Exhibit I-2.

Where the other forms of planning depicted in Exhibit I-1 are more proactive in their approach to achieving institutional goals and objectives, operational planning tends to be more reactive because of the relatively short time frame left to accomplish these goals and objectives. Operational planning also is especially useful and applicable to accomplishing complex projects of a sensitive or critical nature. All colleges experience such projects. For example, a pending visit by the governor to dedicate a new building on your campus could require an operational plan. A well thought out, written operational plan identifies the necessary preparations, a se-

EXHIBIT I-2

Example of an Operational Planning Application

Goal: To increase the college's cash reserve by five percent over the previous year.

Condition: Lower than predicted enrollment is responsible for lower than predicted revenue from tuition.

Strategy: Develop a financial plan for the remaining six months of the fiscal year to reduce expenditures to achieve the five percent cash reserve goal.

---

quence of events, a detailed list of the necessary tasks in support of the event, and the person or office responsible for those tasks. A written operational plan is like an "assurance policy" that the college will avoid a public relations miscue and avoid embarrassment. Albeit, developing an operational plan in this example would prove time consuming; nevertheless, a breach of protocol, failure to consider a foul weather alternative, or some other serious miscue might result in consequences of a much longer duration than it would take to develop such a plan.

Tactical planning, borrowing from the military, is a calculated, deliberate course of action in response to a temporary situation that may have a detrimental effect on a college's ability to accomplish its long range goals. According to Norris and Poulton's exhibit (Exhibit I-1), tactical planning focuses on a one- to three-year horizon or time period along a planning continuum that goes beyond five years.[7] It, i.e., tactical planning, differs from operational planning in the fact that the latter deals with a situation requiring a more immediate and often short term objective – one to three years – that may prove to be a barrier in accomplishing a longer range, strategic goal. Exhibit I-3 that follows is an application of the criteria underlying the development of a tactical plan. That criteria includes a clearly stated goal with a timeline that extends beyond five years; an adverse situation, if not corrected, that could lead to failure to achieve that goal; and a response, i.e., corrective action over a period of 1-3 years, that should put the process for achieving that goal back on its intended course. The sequence of steps employed in this situation were: (1) recognize a problem exists, (2) clearly define the problem, (3) collect and analyze facts bearing on the problem, (4) develop alternative solutions, (5) analyze the alternatives, and (6) decide on the alternative that will best resolve the more immediate issue and, as much as possible, preserve the original goal.

One of the shortcomings of tactical planning among key decision makers is their becoming narrowly focused on resolving the more immediate issue and losing sight of the longer term goal. The euphoria of fighting the battle, i.e., solving the problem, often can become the reason for losing sight of what was originally intended. Too often, the hasty resolution of one problem leads to the creation of another.

Mid-range planning, as noted in Exhibit I-1, spans the gap between tactical and long term planning, i.e., the 3-5 years horizon. Sometimes confused with tactical planning, mid-range plans are more goal oriented and less issue oriented than tactical plans. Where tactical plans seek to resolve an emerging but more imme-

EXHIBIT I-3

Example of a [Tactical] Planning Application

STRATEGIC GOAL: Achieve full and unconditional accreditation for the college's Business Administration program by the Association to Advance Collegiate Schools of Business not later than June 2008.

ADVERSE SITUATION: Accreditation standard requires all faculty have at least a masters degree in the discipline. The college faculty, who are mostly tenured, do not qualify.

RESPONSE: Develop a [tactical] plan that provides for a three-year financial incentive for faculty to meet that standard and provides criteria for employing future faculty in the Business Department.

diate issue, mid-range plans focus on the goal and a more stable approach (3-5 years) to reaching that goal. Generally, community colleges have engaged more in long term (5-10 years) and strategic (10+ years) planning over the last thirty years because that is, or was, more or less a legacy inherited from the traditional four year college and university. Perhaps, long term and strategic planning were more appropriate for the developing years of the community college movement to ensure their place in higher education. However, this is no longer true. Community colleges are here to stay! In today's fast paced, high tech environment, change is almost constant.

Business and industry have adopted mid-range planning as the preferred mode for setting future goals. Because community colleges are a business, i.e., in the business of educating and training, and because a major part of the community college mission is workforce development, community colleges have to be aware of and sensitive to this changing environment. Mid-range planning is adaptable and useful in dealing with change. The 3-5 year planning cycle reduces both the time horizon and the unknown into a manageable process. Environmental scanning in terms of this limited time horizon results in more accurate predictability thus making mid-range planning more effective and more useful. Because goals in mid-range plans are generally limited to the 3-5 years time horizon, target dates for accomplishing objectives leading to goal achievement are within sight, and adjustments in the path leading to goal achievement can be made more easily. Community colleges are known for their adaptability and ability to accommodate change. Long term trends, for the most part, are not considered as being 3-5 years. Mid-range planning fits this 21st century profile and is the recommended mode for dealing with change in a manageable way.

Long term planning generally focuses on setting goals 5-10 years into the future. In today's environment, long term planning is more comparable to strategic planning than mid-range planning because the degree of uncertainty and speculation is considered higher. Environmental scanning, for example, is not a reliable tool for use in long term planning because the information is somewhat limited, and what is available could be highly speculative. For most business and industry, long term planning is more visionary and focuses more on how the organization would like to see itself than on its actual capabilities and abilities to accomplish the long term goals it has set.

Strategic planning is synonymous with long term planning and the two terms are casually intermingled whenever planning processes are the topic for discussion. In the classical sense, strategic planning focuses on goal setting for a period beyond 10 years and as many as 20-25 years in the future. In the context of today's environment, any planning beyond five years is viewed as strategic planning. Traditionally, colleges and universities have used strategic planning models to plot their futures. Often the resulting strategic plans prove useful when institutions are undergoing evaluation for accreditation because the plans fulfill the requirement to show evidence that planning is occurring and that various college constituencies are involved in the planning process. Beyond that, strategic plans most often gather dust on the shelves of administrators because the goals are either no longer relevant, the governing boards have changed direction or the people who developed the plans and led the efforts are no longer connected with or employed at the college.

Summary

Operational planning is a response to today's crisis with the objective of resolving that crisis either permanently or temporarily, buying the time to develop more permanent solutions. This type of planning is most useful in correcting minor deviations that decision makers encounter along the path to accomplishing the college's goals. Tactical planning, on the other hand, is a more deliberate course of action of longer duration to correct a situation that would have a detrimental effect on the college's ability to achieve its goals. Borrowing from the military, college administrations would most likely use operational planning to capitalize on targets of opportunity and to deal with threats to goal achievement while tactical planning looks to a course of action of a longer duration. When an organization – a community college – looks toward its future beyond three years, it engages itself in either mid-range, long term or strategic planning. Mid-range planning is fast becoming the planning model of choice among business, industrial and nonprofit organizations. The latter includes community colleges. What makes mid-range planning a more effective model for change is that it reduces the time horizon, and thus the unknown, into a manageable process. Setting goals for the next 3-5 years is based on environmental factors that are more accurate and predictable. In long term and strategic planning – the terms are interchangeable – the institution is looking beyond five or ten years into the future and thus must rely on factors that are less predictable and, to some degree, highly speculative. Mid-range plan goals of 3-5 years in the future will have target dates for accomplishing the objectives leading to that goal well in sight. Therefore, necessary adjustments because of unforeseen circumstances tend to be more accurate and made more easily. This makes handling change more manageable. Mid-range planning is well-adapted to deal with the fast paced, high tech environment of the 21st century. Because community colleges are characterized as being highly flexible and quickly responsive to change, mid-range planning offers decision makers a process that includes goal stability while retaining the flexibility to react to more immediate issues that might jeopardize goal attainment.

FOOTNOTES

1. William Morris (ed). *The American Heritage Dictionary of the English Language.*

2. George A. Steiner. *Top Management Planning.* p.7

3. Ibid., p. 20

4. Donald M. Norris and Nick L. Poulton. *A Guide for New Planners,* p. 11

5. Authors' note. The bracketed term [MID-RANGE] is not part of Exhibit I-1 as it appears on p. 11 of *A Guide for New Planners.* The bracketed term was added by the authors and will be discussed throughout the text of this publication.

6. Ibid., p. 9.

7. Ibid., p. 11

1

Where It Begins ... Developing a Mission, Purpose and Vision for Your College

- Writing a mission statement that conveys the institution's purpose
- Ten questions to help form, review or revise the college mission statement
- Writing or revising the mission statement — a step-by-step process
- Pitfalls to avoid in the mission statement
- Developing purpose statements that effectively support the college mission
- Creating a vision for success

Writing a Mission Statement That Conveys the Institution's Purpose

"Write down the revelation and make it plain on tablets so that a herald may run with it." This Old Testament quotation clearly points out the importance of writing down a plan or vision so that others may understand and follow it. This is appropriately applied to the development, writing, and revision of the college mission statement. The mission statement serves as the cornerstone in the institutional planning process. It articulates the college's primary purpose for existence and sets the tone for the organization. This public statement communicates, to internal and external audiences, the college's primary purpose for existence, e.g., student learning, and the focus of its effort, to aid in the cultural, economic and intellectual development of its service area. The ultimate purpose of the mission statement is to provide, in writing, not only the chief focus of the college but to engage others to fulfill it.

Higher education veterans have learned a great deal from the corporate world about crafting effective mission statements. In the 1980s and early 1990s there was a resurgence of the importance of the mission statement by both public and private organizations.

Increased competition, changing markets, a sluggish economy and other factors caused business and organization leaders to more closely examine their operations, reprioritize their efforts and refine their focus. Community colleges were and are no different. Changing federal, state and accrediting agency regulations and criteria; declining state aid; shrinking service areas; increased technology costs; changing student populations; and a myriad of other factors have caused community colleges to reconsider their missions.

The mission statement provides the institution the foundation necessary to adjust its direction while maintaining its primary focus. Five major benefits can be derived from an effectively written mission statement. They include:

- Direction — a clear statement of what the organization does and the arenas in which it is to be successful;
- Focus — a description of the institution's strengths and competitive advantages and a prescription for accessing them;
- Policy — a guideline of what an institution finds acceptable and unacceptable and a statement of organizational values;
- Challenge — a basis for goals and measurements established to be achieved by the employees;
- Passion — a source of enthusiasm, pride and commitment felt by everyone involved with the institution.[1]

Even with these compelling benefits, many institutions fail to recognize the importance and utility of a mission statement. Without a clear mission, the planning process cannot be coordinated and cannot generate focused goals and strategies.

Because the mission statement is the foundation for planning, it is important that institution leaders regularly review it to ensure that it effectively communicates the college's primary intent. Many processes have been described to create, review and revise the mission statement. The process selected by the institution must fit its current planning processes and operational framework. One simple process for creating, revising or reviewing a mission statement is to consider a series of questions designed to bring the institution's aspirations clearly into focus. Institution leaders will need to determine how they will answer these questions and which college constituents will be involved in this process. The responses are then used to formulate or revise the mission statement. The more input gathered from college constituents — board, administration, students, faculty, staff, and community members — the more useful and effective the mission will be. Without input from a wide representation of college stakeholders, there is apt to be little acceptance of what the college intends to become or accomplish.

Ten questions have been developed by the authors to guide colleges in the formation, or revision of their mission statements. These questions, along with sample responses, will help the institution sharpen its primary purpose and communicate it more clearly.

Ten Questions to Help Form, Review or Revise the College Mission Statement

1. Who are we? (Example — We are a two-year, public community college.)
2. What do we do? (Example —We enhance student learning and entry-level job skills by providing students associate of science, associate of applied science degrees, and certificate programs that enable them to transfer to another college or university or enter the workforce.)
3. Whom do we serve? (Example —We serve traditional, non-traditional, and high school students.)
4. What is our market area? (Example — Our primary market area consists of a seven-county region in south-central Kansas. As a member of a consortium made up of six community colleges in south-central and western Kansas, we are able to offer courses and degree programs online. Because of our participation in the consortium, our market can be expanded throughout the state of Kansas, the United States, and even foreign countries.)
5. What are our institutional priorities? (Example — Student learning, quality instruction, current technology for instruction, and excellent customer (student) service.)
6. What do we offer? (Example — We offer a well-rounded general education curriculum, two-year associate degrees designed to transfer to state colleges and universities, two-year associate of applied degrees that prepare students in a variety of career choices, business and industry training, student academic support services, and academic and career counseling.)

7. How do we intend to offer our educational programs and services? (Example — We intend to offer our educational programs and services with excellence — utilizing highly trained, qualified professionals. We will measure the effectiveness of our educational programs and services through a sound assessment process.)

8. What is our philosophy? (Example — Our basic philosophy is access — providing educational opportunities for all students and ensuring that all students who desire to attend our college are provided every opportunity to succeed.)

9. What makes our college unique and differentiates it from other competing colleges of our size? (Example — Our college offers free tuition to local high school graduates for the first year and at a reduced rate for the second year. We actively recruit international students and have a growing international student body.)

10. What challenges are we currently facing? What areas will continue to be a challenge for years to come? (Our challenges include state funding, decreasing population in service area, declining enrollments in some major programs of study, and aging facilities.)

One of the most important aspects of this process is engaging college constituents. Current structures within the college should be examined to determine their ability to support and facilitate this process. Three suggested methods have been highlighted below to provide the college some direction on how the questions might be most effectively addressed.

- Questions may be incorporated into a formal survey and distributed to randomly selected constituents of the college which may include students, faculty, staff, administration, Board and community members. Once responses have been completed, they can then be compiled into a draft mission. The college may want to appoint a small committee to draft a mission statement based on the responses.
- Questions can be used as discussion points in a Board planning session. These questions will help improve the focus of the Board and other planning participants. Outcomes from

the discussion can then be used to create a new mission statement or revise the existing one.

- The questions may be used by the Board to direct the administration and other selected constituents to prepare a new mission or recommend revisions to the current one. The responses to the questions can be used to help guide this process.

Writing or Revising the Mission Statement – A Step-by-Step Process

Seldom does a community college board of trustees or administration have the opportunity to craft a first-time mission statement. The "glory days" of building community college districts from the ground up have all but come to an end. And, for the hundreds of existing community colleges, time marches on and the future is now. Just as the times change, so do colleges. The complexities of a transforming society and today's revolutionary technological changes are forcing community colleges to reexamine their missions. Getting started in this process of reexamination is often perplexing. The steps outlined below provide not only a starting point, but also outline a clearly crafted step-by-step process for redefining the mission.

STEP ONE: Answer the ten questions as thoroughly and as thoughtfully as possible. Brainstorm all the possible responses and write them down as they are generated by the stakeholders. If a survey instrument is used, the focus of this step is to develop the survey instrument so that the questions are written clearly and allow participants the opportunity to express themselves freely in their responses.

STEP TWO: Compile the responses into a draft mission statement. Initially, the draft statement may be a page or two long. The primary objective of this step is to capture all of the details from the responses to the questions on paper.

STEP THREE: Spend time editing the responses. It may require several days to edit the responses into the final mission statement form. Ideally, it will consist of only three to four sentences — a brief paragraph. As the writing or revising process begins, keep in mind the following highlighted points:

- Use language that is directed to the target audience and reflects the makeup of the institution.[2]
- "A mission statement should be written to encourage commitment and to energize all employees toward fulfilling the mission."[3]
- Economize on words. They should be clear, concise, effectual and significant.
- The tone of the mission statement should reflect the institution's belief in itself and its purpose.

STEP FOUR: Provide constituents the opportunity to review the near-final draft and make comments. If necessary, additional editing may be needed at this point to further clarify and hone the final mission statement.

STEP FIVE: The final mission statement should be presented to the Board for approval. A brief description of the process used to write or revise the mission statement should be presented.

STEP SIX: The final mission statement should be published and communicated broadly. It should be included in the college catalog and other pertinent publications, such as the institution's strategic plan, annual report, college brochures and employee handbooks. It should be displayed in prominent places on the college campus. The administration should develop strategies to incorporate the mission into its everyday operations.

Pitfalls To Avoid in the College Mission Statement

When writing or revising a mission statement, some pitfalls must be avoided by every institution. If these pitfalls do occur, the mission of the institution may become misdirected, misunderstood and ineffective in guiding the institution to achieve its potential. Some of the most common pitfalls include:
- Allowing humor, sarcasm, and cynicism in the mission statement.
- Generally stating the institution's greatness, what great quality and what great service it provides. (Highlight unique institutional traits.)
- Making lofty statements that have little credibility. (Keep

statements direct, powerful and reasonable.)
- Faking emotion. (If you don't believe it, don't include it.)
- Lying. (Do exactly what you say you're going to do.)
- Failing to incorporate the mission statement into all aspects of the college's business.[2,5]

Developing Purpose Statements that Help to Effectively Fulfill the College Mission

What are purpose statements?

Purpose statements provide the detail to more clearly describe how the mission of the college will be fulfilled. Common themes often found in community college purpose statements include (but are not limited to): the general education core curriculum, student services, developmental education, business and industry training, economic development, outcomes assessment, and lifelong learning. These statements are crucial in the planning process because they enable the institution to clearly link goals and strategies directly to the mission, and they identify key functions of the college that will support goal attainment. If purpose statements are not present, it is difficult to demonstrate how goals are directly linked to the mission and what functional areas of the college are responsible for attaining the goals.

A sample mission with supporting purpose statements follows:

MISSION STATEMENT

XYZ Community College is a student learning centered public institution of higher education that grants associate degrees and occupational certificates. The mission is to seek maximum student learning through high-quality instruction and services that meet the educational and occupational training needs of students and regional business and industry, while providing activities for lifetime enrichment of our students and citizens in south central Kansas and beyond.

STATEMENT OF INSTITUTIONAL PURPOSE

Striving for excellence, XYZ Community College has publicly adopted the following specific institutional purposes:

1. Provide associate degree programs consisting of a general education core and other courses that satisfy lower division requirements of selected baccalaureate programs.
2. Provide associate degree and certificate programs consisting of a general education core and other courses that qualify students for employment.
3. Provide continuing education courses that respond to more immediate career and personal learning needs.
4. Provide educational programs and services such as adult basic education, remedial/developmental education, and accelerated learning experiences that advance student achievement.
5. Provide academic and support services that respond to personal, social and career planning needs of students.
6. Provide customized training and services that assist businesses/industry and aid promotion of economic development.
7. Provide educational, social and cultural programs that address responsible citizenship and are intended to improve the quality of life best in a richly diverse intellectual and social environment.

It is evident that the mission of this college focuses on student learning, quality instruction and services, and meeting the educational and occupational training needs of constituents. The supporting purposes — associate degree programs designed for transfer and employment, continuing education, customized training, and educational, social and cultural programs — all support and help the college fulfill its mission.

As the planning process develops, goals that address key issues and challenges of the institution should be linked specifically to one or more of the institutional purposes, or to the overall mission. Sample goals and their attendant purpose statements have been highlighted in Exhibit 1-1 on the following page to illustrate how college goals can be linked to the mission and purposes.

If the goal does not directly support the overall mission or any of the institutional purposes, the institution should reevaluate its appropriateness.

EXHIBIT 1-1

GOAL	PURPOSE STATEMENT
1. Implement initiatives to improve student performance on learning outcomes in the developmental studies program.	*Provide educational programs and services, such as adult basic education, remedial/developmental education, and accelerated learning experiences, that advance student achievement.*
2. Integrate updated software technology into the daily operations of the Career Guidance and Personal Counseling Center.	*Provide academic and support services that respond to personal, social and career planning needs of students.*
3. Provide support for technology-reliant college degree programs and courses offered on the main campus and at off-site locations.	*Provide associate degree programs consisting of a general education core and other courses that satisfy lower division requirements of selected baccalaureate programs.* *Provide associate degree and certificate programs consisting of a general education core and other courses that qualify students for employment.* *Provide academic and support services that respond to personal, social and career planning needs of students.*

Creating a Vision for Success

"The most pathetic person in the world is someone who has sight, but has no vision." This statement made by Helen Keller not only speaks to individuals, but also portrays the condition of a college without a clear vision.

The vision statement provides the institution the opportunity to dream. This important document presents a vivid and futuristic description of potential markets served, technologies employed, courses and degrees provided, student populations served and the optimum external and internal operating environment. Using the vision statement as a motivational tool will help to generate ongoing action by college leaders and staff to pursue the mission and eventually achieve the institution's potential.

Many colleges have chosen to combine their mission, vision and values into one statement. A common criticism of this approach is that the combined statement often confuses the mission and vision of the college, making it difficult to determine where the mission ends and the vision begins. As stated earlier in this chapter, the mission identifies what the institution does — its primary purpose. The vision of the institution should reflect its ideal and final state of being and should be written so that it conveys the institution's most lofty achievement.

Publishing separate mission, purpose, and vision statements provides the institution clear direction for the planning process. Separate communication of what the institution intends to do, how it will do it, and what it strives to achieve for the future is more effective. Each of these documents is unique and plays a distinct role in the planning process. When they are combined, the intent, scope and vision for the future of the institution is often lost.

Developing a Vision Statement — A Step-by-Step Process

The creation of a vision begins with and relies on institutional faculty, staff and key stakeholders to dream about what the future institution will look like and how it will function. By following the steps below, better assures that the vision that is developed is one that is shared by all stakeholders of the institution.

STEP ONE: During a planning retreat, staff meeting or board meeting, engage three or four small groups comprised of faculty, staff, administrators, board members and community leaders to develop a vision statement. A time frame of five to ten years should be established for the groups to base their visioning process.

STEP TWO: The worksheet in Exhibit 1-4 on page 16 can be used to help the groups work through the visioning process. Additional questions, such as, "How do you want your college to be different?" "What role do you want your college to play in the community?" "What will a successful community college look like?" and other questions may be added to the list outlined on the worksheet. Allow at least one hour for the groups to work through the visioning process.

STEP THREE: Convene the small groups and utilize the worksheet in Exhibit 1-4 to compile the responses. On flip chart pages, organize the responses for each question. After the responses are compiled, prepare a new flip chart page for each question that high-lights the common themes. Display the pages of all the responses to each question and the common themes for each so that all participants may review.

STEP FOUR: The facilitator will then go through each of the questions and confirm the common themes with the entire group. Allow time for discussion to clarify and entertain other ideas that may emerge. New areas should be noted on the flip chart pages. After this has been done for each question, the facilitator should then appoint one or two people to draft a vision statement based on the group's responses and discussion.

STEP FIVE: After the draft vision statement is prepared, it should then be circulated to all participants for review. Revisions will be incorporated by the writer and then distributed again for review until a vision statement is formed that participants can agree on and institutional leaders can enthusiastically support.

Summary

The vision and mission statements are critical to establishing an effective mid-range planning process. The vision creates a vivid and futuristic description of the institution and should challenge and inspire college stakeholders to achieve its mission. While the vision statement drives the institution toward the future, the mission statement serves as the cornerstone in the institutional planning process by clearly articulating its primary purpose for existing. Without a clear vision and a concise mission, an institution cannot effectively plan to meet its current and future needs.

EXHIBIT 1-2

MISSION STATEMENT DEVELOPMENT
OR REVISION WORKSHEET

The mission statement of the institution should clearly articulate its primary purpose. After responding to the questions below, compile and condense responses into a draft mission statement.

1. Who are we?

2. What do we do?

3. Whom do we serve?

4. What is our market area?

5. What are our institutional priorities?

6. What do we offer?

7. How do we intend to offer our educational programs and services?

8. What is our philosophy?

9. What makes our college unique and differentiates it from other competing colleges of our size?

10. What challenges are we currently facing? What areas will continue to be a challenge for years to come?

EXHIBIT 1-2 *(continued)*

ADDITIONAL QUESTIONS:

a. What is our current mission statement?

b. Does our current mission statement still reflect our primary purpose? Is it outdated?

c. What changes in the mission statement should be made?

Formulate the draft or revised mission statement below.

_____

_____

_____

_____

_____

_____

_____

EXHIBIT 1-3

DEVELOPING PURPOSE STATEMENTS

Purpose statements provide more detail that will help the institution attain its mission.

1. Place a check mark beside the functions identified below that describe your college.

FUNCTION	Function Exists
Offer associate degree programs...	☐
Provide a general education curriculum	☐
Provide business and industry training	☐
Offer occupational and technical education programs	☐
Participate in economic development in the service area/region	☐
Provide developmental/remedial education	☐
Provide continuing education opportunities	☐
Provide adult basic education	☐
Provide work-force development opportunities	☐
Provide academic support services for students	☐
Conduct institutional and student outcomes assessment	☐
Offer community services—social, cultural, educational programs ..	☐
Provide a Small Business Development Center	☐
Offer comprehensive student services	☐
Provide distance learning opportunities	☐

2. Identify on the following lines each function checked above and write a brief sentence defining each one.

SAMPLE: *Provide business and industry training. XYZ Community College provides customized training, services and consultation to area businesses and industries.*

EXHIBIT 1-3 *(continued)*

a. _____

b. _____

c. _____

d. _____

e. _____

f. _____

g. _____

h. _____

3. Revise each of the statements drafted in Number 2 so that they are written clearly, concisely and convey the purposes accurately.

a. _____

b. _____

c. _____

d. _____

e. _____

f. _____

g. _____

h. _____

EXHIBIT 1-4

DEVELOPING A VISION STATEMENT

The vision statement provides a vivid and futuristic description of the organization as it achieves its full potential.

Directions: Answer the following questions as completely and thoroughly as possible.

State the institution's mission:

Describe future degree programs and other services that will be offered:

Describe the standards for employees' professional and ethical conduct within and outside of the college:

Describe the college's leadership roles in the community, service area, state and nation:

Describe the college's future partnerships and alliances with government, business and industry, and other educational institutions:

EXHIBIT 1-4 *(continued)*

Describe the external operating environment of the institution:

Describe the internal governing and decision-making processes of the institution:

Describe how future technology will be used to enhance educational courses, programs and services provided to students:

Formulate the responses to the questions into a draft vision statement below:

_____

_____

_____

_____

_____

_____

_____

FOOTNOTES

1. "Thinking Ahead." Dec. 1998, *Restaurant Hospitality, v. 82, pg. 41-43.* [Online] www.web1.infotrac.galegroup.com.

2. Abrahams, Jeffrey. 1995. The Mission Statement Book: 301 Corporate mission Statements from America's Top Companies. Berkeley, California: Ten Speed Press.

3. Stone, Romuald. Winter 1996. "Mission Statements Revisited." *SAM Advanced Management Journal.* v. 61, n1, pp. 31-37. [Online] www.web1.infotrac.galegroup.com

4. "How to Create and Use A Mission Statement." 1997. [Online] www.dealconsulting.com/strategy/mission.html.

5. Jones, Patricia and Larry Kahaner. *Say It and Live It: 50 Corporate Mission Statements that Hit the Mark.*

2
What It Takes ... The Trustees' Role in Developing the College Plan

- Planning manages change
- Legitimizing the board's planning role
- Differentiating roles – board vs. administration
- Making the process work

Planning Manages Change

Business, industry, education and health care are not the same today as they were five or ten years ago, and what we know today will have changed considerably over the next few years. Back in 1986 in his *Handbook for Community and Technical College Trustees,* George Potter wrote:

> Conditions affecting our institutions are changing and changing rapidly .... Enrollments are leveling off in many institutions and even declining in a few. Our once passive student bodies are now making demands regarding almost every aspect of campus life. Statewide coordinating boards are encroaching more and more on the authority of local boards. Governors, legislatures and the public at large are demanding greater accountability not only for how we spend tax monies but the effectiveness, and even value, of our educational programs. Tax dollars, whether from local, state or Federal sources are becoming more scarce.[1]

This was written over 15 years ago. Does all of it sound familiar? Among what boards of trustees have to contend with today are changing Federal and state support for higher education, local taxpayer revolts, changing enrollment patterns from a traditional to a nontraditional student base, changing technology, changing faculty attitudes – change, change and more change! In today's change-happy environment, community colleges can survive only if they can successfully manage change. Those boards of trustees that can't manage change well enough to lead the progress and growth of their colleges will find themselves stagnating and their colleges unable to compete in today's fast paced environment. "As the rate of change in an organization's task environment increases, new and better ways must be found to understand, anticipate, deal with and monitor changes in the environment. Planning is the key management function for dealing with change in a positive, purposeful way."[2] Planning is the first step in managing change.

Legitimizing the Board's Planning Role

Cyril Houle in his classic treatise *Governing Boards* makes reference to the basis from which the planning role evolves. That basis is the fact that "institutions exist to get something done .... an evident, definable and measurable end. To the extent that the people [on the board] involved share a vision .... a common reference point to which they can turn to in times of division or doubt. But it is often appropriate for a board .... to clarify their own vision by using the best rule of exactness: write it down!"[3] The elements of the vision that Houle refers to are the vision statement and the goals and objectives the board of trustees has agreed upon for the college in the performance of its mission. The written document that serves to provide the clarification Houle refers to is the college's written plan for performing its mission by working to accomplish its goals and objectives over a fixed period of time. Included in the written plan is the board's vision statement which serves as a verbal portrait of what the board wants the college to be when all is said and done. Potter's model board policy outlining trustee responsibilities identifies a necessity for the board to "engage in comprehensive and continuous short and long range planning."[4] To further reinforce the board's responsibility to engage itself in planning for mission accomplishment and to act as an agent of change, Potter identifies a corresponding performance standard: "To call for and approve a specific long-range plan for meeting the objectives of the college."[5] Effective boards have in place policies that require the development, approval, continuous review and updating of a college plan, focusing on programs and budgets keyed to broad goals and supporting objectives, covering periods of five, ten or even twenty years. (See Exhibit 2-1 paragraph 3 at the end of this chapter.) Such plans have generally fostered the growth and development of the more progressive institutions and have aided their efforts to be in step with the synchronous growth and development of the communities served by the institution. "Community college trustees clearly have responsibility for assisting their institutions in setting institutional direction and priorities, and for ensuring that financial allocation of resources are made in accordance with institutional vision, mission and goals."[6] Finally, the planning responsibility and tasking by boards of trustees are often mentioned in enabling legislation or state regulations governing community colleges. Some of the earliest literature dealing with community college governance devotes space to the planning function and the role of the board of trustees. In fact, one of the central themes of the policy governance philosophy advocated by John Carver in his work *Boards That Make a Difference*[7] is the board's responsibility to plan for dealing with the future rather than being preoccupied with the past.

Differentiating Roles – Board vs. Administration

Having legitimized its planning role and responsibility, the next logical step for the board of trustees is to differentiate its role from that of the administration. Where the board identifies its future goals and objectives in broad terms, the administration sets in motion its plans on how to achieve those goals after translating them into operational terms. The board identifies the "what," and the administration determines the "how." The administration determines what resources it will need to provide the results the board of trustees envisions, and the board identifies the means for providing those resources. As a point of illustration, paragraph 3B in the same board policy (Exhibit 2-1) identifies the *what:* "Financial planning, including the establishment of budget parameters and priorities, will be conducted at the annual planning session." In response to that policy, the administration, in this particular instance, determined that budget parameters be defined as the sum of revenues received from property taxes, tuition based on the previous year's enrollment, and instructional grants. In addition, the administration noted that instructional technology, faculty development and expansion of selected instructional programs – all priorities discussed earlier with the board of trustees – would serve as the main topics for discussion and action at the annual planning session. In this practical example, the cost for what the administration envisioned exceeded available revenues, and the Board chose to release funds from its cash reserve rather than reduce or eliminate priorities. It is when these parameters, i.e., the *what* and the *how,* are intermingled that confusion results; it is akin to the dilemma faced by boards of trustees and their administrations in trying to resolve the differences between making policy and administering policy.

Making the Process Work

In its planning role, it is incumbent on the board to seek to clearly connect college resources with community needs. After all, the board represents the community to the college and the college to the community. One recommended strategy is to start the board's planning process with a planning retreat. Participation in the retreat should include a broad representation drawn from the college's service area, e.g., business and civic leadership and foundation board members. College mission and vision statements are not written for perpetuity and should be adjusted to meet community needs. Communities change, and their community colleges must be aware of and sensitive to those changes. Therefore, community input to the board on these topics is invaluable. Combining a planning retreat and a community symposium addressing the college's mission, vision and values is a sure method for the college's board of trustees and administration to hear, analyze and consider what the community sees and thinks of its college and the contributions the college makes to that community. Knowing how much or how little a community values its college provides valuable insight to a board of trustees as it exercises its planning role. Another source of valuable insight to the board is the college foundation. Inclusion of the foundation in the planning process is just another tool the board has to help connect the college to the community. Foundation members are selected because of their interest in the well being of the college and because of their influence and ties to the community. Both the board and the foundation have a common bond; they are working for the betterment of the college.

Visionary boards understand that an effective college is one that is capable of maintaining its stability as well as being able to adapt to change. The planning process goes a long way in helping an institution meet this criteria. Planning is simply predetermining courses of action that help to predict and control the institution's future courses of action. As such, planning contributes to the maintenance of stability because of the control it introduces to future decision-making by the board and subsequently the college's administration. In fact, planning can be referred to as a conscious decision process.

Many planning concepts exist for business, industry and the military, but few such concepts exist that are specifically designed to serve postsecondary education institutions. However, boards of trustees will find that several planning concepts that serve business, industry and the military can be easily adapted to serve their educational institutions. One such concept, though somewhat simplistic, was introduced over thirty years ago and has withstood the test of time. The concept is readily adaptable because it makes use of input from all of the institution's constituencies; it is straight forward and logically sequenced; and it can be incorporated easily into a board's policy governance process without the danger of usurping the administration's prerogatives. In other words, this concept remains in the policymaking domain and incorporates the following principles:[8]

1. **Identify opportunities and anticipate problems.** This principle presumes that the board is somewhat well informed and in touch with the political, economic and social fabric of the community or region that the college serves. A well informed board is actively connected to its community and is very much aware of state and national trends to which its college can react and be responsive. There is no substitute for board education. Board members attendance at state association meetings and their constant interaction with state legislators and congressional delegates help fill the knowledge void. A wealth of information and warnings of dire consequences flow freely from the offices of legislative and congressional staffs.

2. **Establish goals.** This principle relies on input from the community, the board, the administration and other key college constituencies; it considers the information from the preceding

paragraph and integrates that information into the timetable the board sets for achieving these goals. This information helps boards craft goals that are realistic and achievable under current conditions. For example, being warned that the state will face impending shortages in its educational building funds forces the board to look for alternative revenue sources to help solve the college's space problems.

3. **Accumulate information.** Again, this principle depends wholly on several sources – those mentioned in paragraph two plus information about the future environment available from state and Federal agencies. Board members can also accumulate information by attending state trustee conferences, national and regional ACCT meetings, and from a host of publications such as the *Trustee Quarterly,* the *Community College Journal* and the *Chronicle of Higher Education.*

4. **Establish planning assumptions by forecasting future conditions.** Environmental scanning techniques as used by futurist Ed Barlow and known environmental scanner Joe Lapin are especially valuable.[9] Scanning is nothing more than gathering and analyzing trend information concerning the environment within which the community and the college operate. A myriad of sources of current trend data already exist in usable formats thanks to the glut of information technology and the Internet. Those closest to home include the state's legislative research service, state departments of education, state higher education agencies, and, in growing numbers, state community college associations. On the national level, the Census Bureau generally defines its findings by region and national aggregate data. Also, environmental scanning data are available through the Department of Education and the National Center of Educational Management Systems (NCHEMS). Particularly helpful are source data gathered by the American Association of Community Colleges (AACC), the Association of Community College Trustees (ACCT) and the American Association of Higher Education (AAHE). Based on what these data sources reveal about predicted student demographics, inflation rates, population growth, state revenues, regional wealth, etc., fairly accurate planning assumptions can result. Some examples of sound planning assumptions are:

A. Given the number of students in grade 9 in public and private high schools, the predicted college freshman population in 200X can be expected to decrease by 1.5-2.5 percent.

B. Given that the cost price index (CPI) is expected to rise at an annual rate of 2.5-3.0 percent over the next three years, the college can anticipate increases in tuition and fees of $3-$5 per credit hour.

C. Given that property values are expected to increase as high as ten percent within the next three years because of the new manufacturing plant, the college will purchase adjoining properties for expansion.

5. **Develop and choose among alternative courses of actions.** Targeted objectives leading to goal achievement provide a control mechanism while avoiding the pitfall of managing the process which is the administration's prerogative. Objectives can be thought of as predetermined, sequenced steps to goal achievement. For example: Southern Region Community College will initiate a progressive campaign to increase student enrollment to an annual minimum of 30,000 credit hours by June 30, 2006. Thus, annual credit hour production must increase by at least 3.2 percent using the base enrollment for the 2002-03 school year.

6. **Set priorities.** By selecting and ranking goals that provide mission focus, the board provides the right amount of general guidance that will ultimately lead to the results noted in the college's vision.

7. **Establish policies that assure the existence of an institutional planning process and assure maximum input from a broad array of college constituencies**. To assure that its planning process is not lost among the short term critical issues on which boards generally have to respond, a board policy should be set in place which outlines the minimum requirements to be considered. A sample policy is provided in Exhibit 2-1. In addition, the board should insist on hearing input from its multiple constituencies before approving its planning document.

8. **Establish a mechanism for monitoring progress and for measuring adherence to the college's plan.** The sample board policy at Exhibit 2-1, in its opening paragraph, provides

for "periodically reviewing progress on planned goals and objectives." This takes the form of monitoring reports as reported by Carver in his work on policy governance.[7] A well-written board policy should make specific mention of the need for such monitoring reports. Paragraph 2 of the exhibit clearly specifies that "the primary focus of Board deliberations will be on determining the progress of the college towards achieving results through the use of reports and monitoring reports."[10] The effective board will be able to monitor progress through an accountability mechanism that is linked with executive performance. Exhibit 2-2 at the end of the chapter is an example of how one college links the two units by its very first sentence: "Monitoring executive performance is synonymous with monitoring organizational performance ..."[11] Even though this addresses the monitoring of policy, the same kind of accountability is appropriate for assessing progress on achieving institutional goals.

Summary

In summary, the most effective boards of trustees are those whose philosophy of governance emphasizes a "proactive" rather than a "reactive" approach to accomplishing the college mission now and in the future. Such an approach helps the college influence its future rather than only respond to other forces or react to situations after they have reached the crisis stage. Effective boards, because of their recognition of the legitimacy of their planning role and responsibilities, will find themselves in a position to provide clear answers to two very basic questions: (1) Why are we here? (2) If this is why we are here, what should be accomplished? To help arrive at the answers to these questions, the effective board must have a clear understanding of its responsibility to preserve the institution's future by adopting a strategy that maps the road to its vision for the future. That strategy takes the form of deciding upon a planning concept and implementing a process that translates that concept into action that results in accomplishing the college's goals for the future. That road map takes the form of the college plan, and the goals are what mark the route for the college's board and administration in accomplishing the mission and ultimately achieving the college's vision.

EXHIBIT 2-1

PRATT COMMUNITY COLLEGE BOARD POLICY

Policy No. __1-05__ Policy Type____Governance____
Policy Title ___Board Planning and Agenda___
Date Adopted __3-17-97__
Date Revised __12-21-98__
Date Deleted _____
Review Date ___7-30-01___

The Board will carry out its responsibilities in a manner consistent with Board policies by (a) developing and reviewing Board objectives annually, (b) holding an annual planning session, (c) periodically reviewing progress on planned goals and objectives, and (d) following an agenda at its regular monthly meetings which implements the Board policy on Governing Style.

1. The agenda for all Board meetings will be prepared by the President in consultation with the Board chair and vice chair, based on input from other Board members. The agenda will be prepared and delivered to the Board at least seven (7) days before the meeting.

2. The primary focus of Board deliberations will be on determining the progress of the college towards achieving results, through the use of reports and monitoring data.

3. The annual planning session will be held at least 90 days prior to approval of the annual budget.

   A. The College Mission, purposes, and philosophy will be reviewed at the annual planning session.
   B. Financial planning, including the establishment of budget parameters and priorities, will be conducted at the annual planning session.
   C. Subjects for Board discussion and action during the following year will be developed at the annual planning session.

4. The College budget will be approved by the Board not later than July 25 each year. A revised budget may be submitted at the discretion of the President to the Board for approval during the February Board meeting.

5. Board policies and policy revisions will not be adopted until they have been considered at a minimum of two meetings, unless Board action waives this requirement and immediate effect is authorized.

___This is a new policy.
__X_This replaces policy dated _3-17-97_

EXHIBIT 2-2

PRATT COMMUNITY COLLEGE BOARD POLICY

Policy No. __5-02__ Policy Type__Personnel__
Policy Title __Monitoring Presidential Performance__
Date Adopted __3-17-97__
Date Revised __9-17-01__
Date Deleted _____
Review Date __9-01__

Monitoring executive performance is synonymous with monitoring organizational performance against Board policies on Board objectives, institutional goals and Executive Limitations. The Board will monitor performance in a manner as to have systematic assurance of policy compliance, including accomplishments of goals and objectives.

1. The purpose of monitoring is to determine the degree to which Board policies and objectives are being fulfilled. Monitoring will be done in a way to allow the Board more time to focus on and discuss the future rather than review the past.

2. A given policy may be monitored in one or more of three ways:

   A. INTERNAL REPORTS — Disclosure of compliance information to the Board from the President. Internal reports include:

   - Institutional data collection
                - Community surveys
                - Placement data
                - Assessment of student learning
                - Financial reports
                - Assessment of institutional effectiveness
                - Core Indicators of Quality Improvement

   B. EXTERNAL REPORTS — Disclosure of compliance by an external auditor or other persons or entities external to the institution. External reports include:
                - Audit reports
                - Licensing examination results
                - Accreditation reports
                - Transfer data

   C. DIRECT BOARD INSPECTION — Discovery of compliance information by a Board member, a committee or the Board as a whole. This is an inspection of documents, activities or circumstances

EXHIBIT 2-2 *(continued)*

directed by the Board and/or conducted by an external auditor which allows a test of policy compliance.

3. The information noted above will be considered in the Board's formal, annual evaluation of presidential performance. Such evaluation will occur in December of each year by a method designated by the Board.

   A. The results of the annual performance evaluation shall be discussed with the president by the full Board in January.

   B. The Board shall make a consideration in January relative to the continuation or extension of the President's employment contract and any changes thereto.

___This is a new policy.
_X_ This replaces policy dated _2-17-97_____.

FOOTNOTES

1. George E. Potter, J.D., *Handbook for Community and Technical College Trustees* (Annandale, VA: ACCT, 1986) p. 1.
2. Don Hellriegel and John W. Slocum, *Management: Contingency Approaches* (London: Addison-Wesley, 1988), p. 234.
3. Cyril O. Houle, *Governing Boards* (San Francisco: Jossey-Bass, Inc., 1989) pp. 124-125.
4. Potter, p. 10.
5. Potter, p. 14
6. Jan Balzer, "Trustees Have a Role in Information Technology Strategic Planning," *Trustee Quarterly* (Summer 2001), p. 27.
7. John Carver, *Boards That Make a Difference* (San Francisco: Jossey-Bass, 1990).
8. R. Murdick, "Nature of Planning and Plans," *Advanced Management Journal* 32 (1967) p. 37.
9. Barlow and Lapin are known futurists who keynoted the 1996 ACCT annual convention and provided research for the AACC Commission on the Future of Community Colleges and its classic report "Building Communities."
10. Board Policy 1-05 is taken with permission from *Board of Trustees Policy Manual,* Pratt Community College, Pratt, KS.
11. Board Policy 5-02 is taken with permission from the *Board of Trustees Policy Manual,* Pratt Community College, Pratt, KS.

3

What We Know ... The Environmental Scan and How to Use It Effectively for Mid-Range Planning

- Environmental scanning defined
- Getting started
- Locating relevant information
- From scanning to planning

Community colleges, like business and industry, can attribute their success in the educational marketplace to the vision and support of their boards of trustees and the ability of their senior leadership to adapt quickly to change. Today's rapidly changing high tech environment provides little lead time for key decision makers to analyze the factors driving those changes and to respond accordingly. In the past, college administrations have relied primarily on historical data and performance to provide the basis upon which to build strategic or long range plans. Using historical trend data to build plans merely perpetuates the past and the present. This limits an institution's ability to anticipate change and to adapt to the changing environment in a conscious and systematic manner. Relying too heavily on the past generally results in a reactive rather than a proactive management philosophy. Reaction is the product of surprise, and surprise is the result of not being prepared to deal with unanticipated change. Therefore, to have a proactive management philosophy, an institution must be in a position to deal with change. Environmental scanning is a method to accomplish this. However, the further out one ventures in anticipating change, the less effective will be the ability to predict. This is the greatest shortcoming associated with strategic or long range planning. The risk of under anticipating change is considerably less with the mid-range planning process which in turn, makes environmental scanning more effective.

Environmental Scanning Defined

Environmental scanning is an essential, but often neglected step in the planning process. Unlike most commercial businesses whose goals include making a profit and gaining their share of the market, higher education institutions which are largely nonprofit, i.e., not solely dependent on tuition and fees, do not depend on market share to assure their survivability. Commercial businesses are in a continuous mode of environmental scanning because they continuously plan to meet the demands of the marketplace. Community colleges, which are largely tax supported, often participate – sometimes unknowingly – in environmental scanning when they respond to the workforce development needs of their local communities, their districts/regions and their states. A better understanding of what environmental scanning is all about can sharpen a college's response to the needs of its constituencies. Environmental scanning is the steering mechanism on the college's vehicle for change and the basis for its continuous planning to deal with that change.

A simple definition of environmental scanning is offered by Brown and Weiner in their 1985 publication dealing with change management as "a kind of radar to scan the world systematically and signal the new, the unexpected, the major and the minor."[1] Key words here are *radar, signal* and *unexpected*. The environment in which community colleges must function is a complex set of social, cultural, political and economic conditions affecting the nature of both their service areas and their internal organizations. Like the "radar" suggested by Brown and Weiner, scanning is the process of examining, quickly but thoroughly, the conditions previously noted. Most often, environmental scanning is associated with the external environment. Aguilar, in 1967, wrote that environmental scanning is "… the activity of acquiring information … about events and relationships in a company's [college's] outside environment, the knowledge of which would assist top management in its task of charting the company's future course of action."[2] By being knowledgeable of those external conditions that may force change, community college boards and administrations are in a better position to respond to that change as it develops rather than being caught in the untenable position of having to react to that change after it occurs. Effective scanning puts a board and its administration in position to identify early threats that can negatively influence the college's mission. Furthermore, effective scanning also puts the college in a better position to recognize opportunities that can strengthen the college mission. This, in turn, can help the college to improve its planning process and gain a more competitive advantage in the higher education marketplace.

Many community colleges that engage themselves in environmental scanning as a prelude to planning stop after having reviewed, discussed and analyzed their external environment. They often forget to closely scrutinize what may become of their internal environment as they enter the era of change. While external scanning includes outside environmental factors that can affect the performance of a college, scanning the college's internal environment is necessary to determine if the college has the desire, the attitude and the means to deal with pending changes. Scanning the college's internal environment is defined as acquiring, analyzing and using information about the college's resources – staffing, financial, facilities, etc. In addition, internal scanning includes information about the organizational climate, the college's internal communications and other similarly classified elements/processes that assist the board and administration in determining how the college will proceed. Identifying trends that will affect the college's response to change and taking proactive steps to positively influence the impact of that change will serve as the basis for developing the college's plans for its future.

Getting the Scanning Process Started

Joel Lapin, an external environmental scanner and forecaster, and a research associate with the Commission on the Future of Community Colleges, quoted Jack Welch, then the chief executive officer of General Motors, who said, "When the rate of change on the outside exceeds the rate of change on the inside, the end is in sight." What both Lapin and Welch were alluding to is an organization that is not proactive in adapting to its changing environment will soon lose its competitive edge. Scanning is the first step to becoming proactive. A survey of various planning processes used in education, business, industry, and the military reveals that there is no one generally accepted process for gathering, classifying, analyzing or using information for identifying trends and emerging issues. Trends are characteristics of the college's environment that reflect its cultural, economic, political and technological climate over a period of time. An example of a broad trend is: "the rapid development of emerging technologies is increasing the demand for a highly skilled, well-trained workforce." That increased demand for skilled and well-trained workers is identified as a relevant characteristic that eventually impacts the college mission. Becoming aware of the broader trend – rapid development of emerging technologies – and the relevance of that to the college mission, i.e., developing a highly skilled, well-trained workforce, are examples of the first two steps in environmental scanning. Trends become more meaningful and useful when linked to emerging issues. Take one step further the example of the trend of emerging technologies creating workforce needs and the relevance of that to the college mission; tie that to an event – a congressional committee considering a bill to subsidize tuition for students choosing high tech programs; and an emerging issue is most likely to arise. Lapin defines an emerging issue as "a potential controversy that arises from a trend or event, which may require a response."[4] The most likely response would be the college including in its plan provisions for developing selected high tech programs and steps to generate enrollment using Federal financial aid to attract students. Analysis of pending environmental change through scanning and the development of institutional plans to deal with future change are keys to the college's success.

> "In essence, a college that establishes an environmental scanning and forecasting system has benefits of an early warning system to identify trends and events that, when forecasted, present both threats and opportunities to the college. This system will increase management's efficiency in dealing with uncertainties inherent in the future by anticipating change and influencing the future rather than by simply reacting to it."[5]

Business, industry, and the military are quite effective in using environmental scanning as the basis upon which they build their plans. Discussions with chief executive officers of a variety of corporations and the experience of a former U.S. Air Force chief educational planner indicate more similarities than differences on how they scan. Keeping in mind that environmental scanning is simply gathering and using information about trends in the college's external environment, the relationships of these trends to the college's operations and their projected impact on future operations, the following steps are appropriate:

1. Gather information that identifies broad trends.
2. Determine which of those trends may have relevance to both present and future college operations.
3. Identify sources of critical information on those relevant trends.
4. Collect the critical information.
5. Formulate objectives and strategies.

Information that identifies broad trends can come from a variety of sources – Federal, state and local government officials, community leaders, political strategists, business and industry leadership, professional associations and a host of others. Information sources will be highlighted later in this chapter. Borrowing from Lapin's 1997 presentation, Exhibits 3-1 and 3-2 provide examples of broad and relevant trends identified by two colleges.[6] Without further elaboration, the author of any one of the colleges' plans can relate the trends and their impact to a variety of college operations.

EXHIBIT 3-1

BISMARCK STATE COLLEGE
BISMARCK, ND

A. The Bismarck area population will average a 1.6% growth rate per year through 2010.

B. With fewer young people and their out-migration, the elderly population cohort in North Dakota will increase in the future.

C. There will be a gradual increase in state funding of public schools and post-secondary institutions in North Dakota, with less of the increase going to public colleges.

Exhibit 3-1, paragraph A is an example of a broad trend which alerted Bismarck State College planners to expect a statewide population growth of 16 percent over the ten year period through 2010. Knowing what percentage of the state's population constitutes the college's service area, planners are able to predict the growth in that area. A relevant trend can be found in paragraph B indicating less future growth in the college's primary constituency. Also, paragraph C of the same exhibit is considered a relevant trend indicating an expected funding shortfall during a period of steady growth.

EXHIBIT 3-2

**TRUCKEE-MEADOWS COMMUNITY COLLEGE
RENO, NV**

A. Gaming interests will continue to be the most powerful economic and political force in our community generating the largest number of jobs.

B. Population growth in southern Nevada will have political and financial impacts on northern Nevada in years ahead.

Exhibit 3-2 is an example of broad based trends that would require further exploration to determine their relevancy to future college operations. From these trends, planners might surmise that state revenues from gaming interests that are allocated to the support of higher education would continue to grow; that the need for workforce development to support the gaming industry and travel and tourism would be expected to increase; and that continued population growth will challenge the college to keep pace to service that growth.

The next step in the environmental scanning process, then, is to identify sources of information to help ascertain the relevancy of those trends and their impact on future college operations.

Locating Relevant Information to Support Scanning

Publications provide information, but people provide explanation and insight. The point here is that the best sources of relevant information are face to face discussions with people whose careers and livelihood depend on such information. Governmental officials and their staffs rely heavily on data and their resulting analysis to predict trends that will have a future impact on their constituencies and service functions. Furthermore, government offices generally have the resources to collect and analyze data and to translate it into useful information. That is an important part of their job. Interviewing these officials – Federal, state and local – on future oriented topics such as population growth, mobility trends, the state of the economy, industrial trends and a host of others will produce a wealth of information. Connecting that information to college operations is the next step by asking, "How might that trend impact the future operation of the college?" Responding to that question takes some creative thinking on the part of the board of trustees and college administration. Another excellent source for identifying trends relevant to the future of your community college is information published and distributed by professional and trade oriented associations. The American Association of Community Colleges (AACC), The Association of Community College Trustees (ACCT), and the American Association of Higher Education (AAHE), collect, analyze and report a wide variety of data and information that are very helpful in identifying future trends, their implications and impacts, and suggestions on how to deal with the trends. The Encyclopedia of Associations identifies numerous national associations whose interest impact community colleges and whose publications are helpful in alerting colleges of future trends. The Federal Register and similar publications for every state and the Monthly Catalog of U.S. Government Publications are helpful sources. Focusing directly on the world of academia, the ERIC Document Reproduction Service is especially appropriate. There are several research institutes – "think tanks" – that specialize in environmental scanning and offer free or low cost reports of their analysis. The most popular of these are: American Enterprise Institute for Public Policy Research (Washington, D.C.), Brookings Institute (Washington, D.C.), and the Institute for the Future (Menlo Park, CA). There is no lack of resources for environmental scanning. The difficulty is finding the talent and the time for scanning.

From Scanning to Planning

The leap from scanning to planning is not insurmountable: however, it does require a combination of dedicated resources, commitment on the part of the board of trustees and the college leadership and participation of the faculty and staff. Exhibit 3-3 illustrates the flow of activity from the outset of environmental scanning to the point of readiness to develop the plan. Succeeding chapters deal with actual plan development and linking planning to budgeting, facilities, equipment management and assessment.

The process from scanning to mid-range planning is a seven-step compilation of the information presented throughout this chapter culminating with the development of the mid range plan. These steps include:

1. Identify relevant economic, political, social and technical trends.
2. Analyze, forecast and evaluate the impacts of these trends on the college in terms of the opportunities and the threats those trends present.

These first two steps constitute external environmental scanning as discussed earlier in this chapter.

3. Survey the organizational climate of the college on its readiness and willingness to deal with change and determine the availability and commitment of resources to accommodate change.
4. Analyze the college's mission, strengths and weaknesses to determine how change can be accommodated.

These steps constitute internal environmental scanning. The readiness and willingness of an organization to enter into transformation cannot be overstated. These steps are often overlooked, misjudged or, at best, taken for granted. Change does not come easily and sometimes has to be coerced. The more forceful the coercion is, the greater is the opportunity for failure to change.

5. Project 3-5 years into the future the strengths, weaknesses, opportunities and threats surfaced from both the external and internal scans and synthesize that information in terms of its impact on the college.

6. Using the mission statement as a point of departure, develop a mutually agreed upon vision statement, with input from the community, board and college leadership. That statement should realistically reflect what they want the college to look like, i.e., its "state of being" in the future.
7. Develop the goals and objectives, taking into account the college's climate and resources, that will move the college along the path to successful fulfillment.

The culmination of this process is the compiling, analyzing, synthesizing and recording of this information into a planning document that will be used to guide and monitor college operations over the next five years. The plan, to be truly comprehensive and complete, must address the resources needed to achieve that college vision and must provide for a mechanism to assess and evaluate the outcomes of both the effort engaged and the resources expended. It (the plan) is not complete unless it is directly linked to the college budget and to its assessment processes.

EXHIBIT 3-3

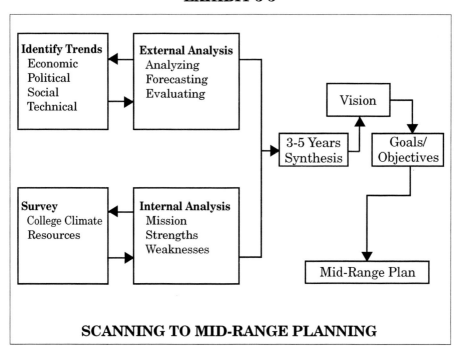

SCANNING TO MID-RANGE PLANNING

Summary

Traditionally, colleges have used historical data to discern trends and to provide a basis for building plans. As a result, colleges have put themselves in the position of reacting to change rather than being proactive in affecting change. Environmental scanning is the gathering of evidence that implies impending change, analyzing that evidence in terms of relevant future trends and their impact on the college, and using that evidence to project opportunities and threats to future college operations. Many colleges engage themselves in scanning without recognizing the process. They are able to identify the more obvious future relevant trends and use that information to their advantage. What colleges often fail to do, however, is to scan their organizational climate to determine if their internal stakeholders are ready and willing to change. Scanning does have its limitations. The farther out one ventures into the future, the less effective scanning will be. That uncertainty can be unnerving and increases the risk of using the resulting projections.

For this reason, scanning is most useful when applied to the mid-range planning process which projects the future 3-5 years hence. Scanning, by itself, is not a difficult process. However, it does take a commitment of time and a resource person to be successful.

A wealth of information exists from which scans can be drawn. Government officials and political leadership at all levels depend on information about future trends to put them in a position to better serve their constituencies. Professional associations produce data and information in easily digested formats. There are numerous Federal and state government publications focused on specific subjects that directly impact college operations. The use of all of these sources in combination generally produce the best results. It was said earlier that publications provide information but people provide insight. There is no substitute for face to face discussions with people whose careers and livelihood depend on such information. Trend analysis, internal and external scanning, information synthesis, creating a vision and formulating goals and objectives to achieve that vision culminate in the development of a planning document – the mid-range plan – to guide future college operations.

FOOTNOTES

1. A. Brown and Erich Weiner. *Supermanaging: How to Harness Change for Personal and Organizational Success.* (New York: Mentor, 1985), p. ix.

2. Francis J. Aguilar. *Scanning the Business Environment.* (New York: Macmillan Company, 1967), p. 1.

3. Joel Lapin, in a presentation "Discovering Your Community's Future Learning Needs," March 19, 1997.

4. Ibid.

5. James L. Morrison and William G. Held. "Developing Environmental Scanning/Forecasting Systems to Augment Community College Planning," VCCA Journal (Spring/Summer 1989), p. 13.

6. Lapin, "Discovering Your Community's Future Learning Needs."

4

Where We Should Go ... Establishing the Mid-Range Planning Process

---

- Understanding the mid-range planning process: an overview

- The board planning survey: where mid-range planning begins

- The board planning session: engaging board, administration, faculty and staff into the planning process

- Establishing the annual planning session agenda

- Developing the planning document

- Communicating the plan

- Establishing and utilizing planning sessions at every level of the institution

Understanding the Mid-Range Planning Process: An Overview

Stephen Covey, in his highly successful book, *The 7 Habits of Highly Effective People,* provides a keen illustration of how planning should be viewed, both in our lives and in institutions. "All things are created twice. There's a mental or first creation, and a physical or second creation of all things. You have to make sure that the blueprint, the first creation, is really what you want, that you've thought everything through. Then you put it into bricks and mortar. Each day you go to the construction shed and pull out the blueprint to get marching orders for the day. You begin with the end in mind."[1]

This excerpt clearly illustrates the importance and value of having a written plan and utilizing it to direct the daily operations of the institution. Unfortunately, many colleges have crafted planning documents that are shelved and unused.

The mid-range planning process described in this chapter provides a mechanism for colleges to establish, pursue, and evaluate progress toward its goals and objectives in an ongoing, systematic manner. This process provides institutions the framework necessary to ensure that planning becomes part of the regular operation of the institution. In achieving established goals, a college develops a solid foundation for future budgeting, operations, assessment, facilities and equipment planning. Once a comprehensive and continuous planning process has been established, faculty, staff, administration and the board will see meaningful benefits. These benefits include: 1) stability in college operations, 2) improved communication within the institution, 3) a mechanism to address unforeseen situations and 4) improved communications with external constituencies.

As the name implies, the mid-range planning process bridges the middle years in the continuum, as illustrated in Exhibit 4-1.

EXHIBIT 4-1

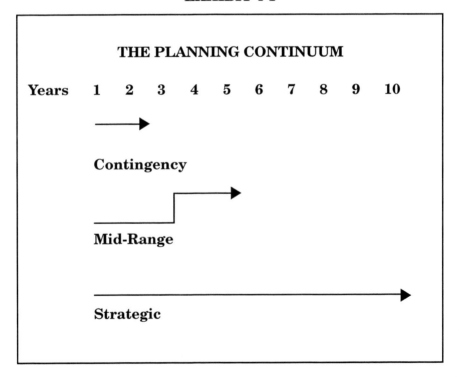

THE PLANNING CONTINUUM

Years   1   2   3   4   5   6   7   8   9   10

Contingency

Mid-Range

Strategic

One thing is certain — all planning is risky and uncertain. A corporate manager summed it up best when he said, "No amount of sophistication is going to allay the fact that all your knowledge is about the past and all your decisions are about the future."[2] Contingency, or tactical plans, prescribe ready responses to conditions that are imminent while strategic plans generally contemplate a 10-year horizon. Mid-range planning links the opposite ends of the continuum, and therefore entails less uncertainty and more reasonable risk. The effectiveness of mid-range planning is increased when the process is driven by continuous updating and replanning based on changing conditions. When this pattern is followed, planning becomes a routine way of life for the top and middle echelons of leadership and faculty.

The Board Planning Survey:
Where Mid-Range Planning Begins

A college's board of trustees is the power base of its leadership and the primary impetus for its future vision. As such, the board must be integrated into the initial phases of planning. In order for a college to establish and maintain a solid planning foundation, the board of trustees, and the administration must clearly identify issues that challenge the institution. As discussed in Chapter 3, the environmental scan provides the institution information necessary to identify current issues, trends and challenges important to the future of the college. The board also must be able to articulate desired outcomes and establish priorities for addressing the challenges and opportunities.

A well-designed survey instrument can capture the board's perception of the importance and priority of various issues as well as the value they place on each institutional outcome. Two sample surveys are included in Exhibits 4-2 and 4-3 of this chapter as examples to help the board survey process.

The Planning Process Effectiveness Survey, (Exhibit 4-2) was designed to improve the institution's current planning process by identifying strengths and weaknesses. Institutions that have a planning process in place but desire to improve its effectiveness may benefit from this tool.

EXHIBIT 4-2

PLANNING PROCESS EFFECTIVENESS SURVEY

The purpose of this survey is to gather information from the Board of Trustees to identify strengths, weaknesses and issues of concern regarding the current planning process. Results of this survey will be used to develop the agenda and discussion sessions for the upcoming planning retreat. Your answers will be treated confidentially and will be compiled with other board members' responses. Please return the completed survey no later than January 15, 2005. Thank you for your input!

In your opinion, how often have the following planning functions occurred?
1=Always 2=Regularly 3=Rarely 4=Never 5=No Opinion

1 2 3 4 5   The college mission, purpose statements and vision are reviewed by the Board of Trustees.

1 2 3 4 5   The president exhibits the appropriate vision, leadership and commitment to the strategic planning process.

1 2 3 4 5   The administrative team exhibits the necessary commitment to the planning process.

1 2 3 4 5   Internal and external environmental scan data and other assessment data is reviewed by the Board to help establish a foundation for planning.

1 2 3 4 5   Key issues and challenges faced by the institution are discussed by the administration and the Board, and strategies to address these situations are incorporated into the institutional plan.

1 2 3 4 5   The Board of Trustees has direct input into the planning process of the institution.

1 2 3 4 5   Faculty and staff provide input into the development of goals of the college.

1 2 3 4 5   The Board receives timely, accurate reports (oral or written) on the progress toward the goals identified in the plan.

EXHIBIT 4-2 *(continued)*

Please rate your level of knowledge and understanding of the following planning functions.

    1 = Very knowledgeable/high level of understanding
    2 = Little knowledge or understanding
    3 = No knowledge or understanding

1 2 3 The relationship of the college mission to the overall planning process.

1 2 3 How the institutional planning process works.

1 2 3 The benefits of planning for the institution.

1 2 3 How external and internal environmental scan data and other research data is used to help guide the planning process and goal development.

1 2 3 How faculty and staff input is gathered and utilized in goal development.

1 2 3 The role of the administration in the management of the planning process.

1 2 3 How the planning and budgeting processes are linked.

1 2 3 Provisions or procedures for evaluating the planning process.

How do you view the Board of Trustees involvement in the following aspects of the planning process?

1=Very involved 2=Limited involvement 3=No involvement

1 2 3 Review and revision of the college mission, purpose and vision statements.

1 2 3 Monitoring goals of the institutional plan to ensure that they support the vision, mission and purposes of the college.

1 2 3 Development of key issues and challenges facing the college.

1 2 3 Management of the institution's plan.

1 2 3 Determination of budget priorities that support institutional goals.

EXHIBIT 4-2 *(continued)*

1. **In your opinion, what are the major strengths of the current planning process?**

_____

_____

_____

2. **In your opinion, what are the major problems with the current planning process?**

_____

_____

_____

3. **What action needs to take place to correct the problems identified in question two?**

_____

_____

This survey is most effective when implemented prior to the start of the planning cycle, so that strengths and weaknesses of the current process can be identified and addressed. The institution may desire to administer this survey every few years to gauge the board's perception of the usefulness and effectiveness of the planning process and to monitor improvements.

At the onset of the planning cycle, the institution should administer the Board Planning Session Survey. This survey should be sent to each board member and the results anonymously compiled. The Board Planning Session Survey (Exhibit 4-3) is designed to help the institution identify and articulate key issues and goals. This survey should be conducted at the start of the planning cycle, prior to the annual board planning session. The responses help to provide direction to the college president and the administration as they prepare for the annual board planning session.

EXHIBIT 4-3

BOARD PLANNING SESSION SURVEY

In an effort to continually improve the planning process at our institution, your input is essential. To set the foundation for the upcoming annual Board planning session, please indicate the level of importance — from your personal viewpoint — by circling the number that best describes your feelings toward the key issues below.

KEY ISSUES TO BE ADDRESSED

	Very Important	Important	Neutral	Little Importance	No Importance
1. Institution's responsiveness in meeting student needs.	5	4	3	2	1
2. Increasing class offerings at non-traditional times.	5	4	3	2	1
3. Tailoring class offerings to meet the demands/ needs of students	5	4	3	2	1
4. Improving customer service across the institution.	5	4	3	2	1
5. Pursuing more aggressively non-traditional, electronic modes of course/program delivery (i.e., Internet, inter-active TV).	5	4	3	2	1
6. Examining more closely reasons for student failure in courses.	5	4	3	2	1
7. Upgrading technology across the campus.	5	4	3	2	1
8. Initiating more aggressive efforts to attract non-traditional students.	5	4	3	2	1
9. Recognizing teaching excellence.	5	4	3	2	1

EXHIBIT 4-3 *(continued)*

Please indicate the level of importance by circling the number that best describes your feelings toward pursing the future initiatives listed below.

FUTURE INITIATIVES

	Very Important	Important	Neutral	Little Importance	No Importance
1. Pursuing a regional or state-wide collaboration with other community colleges to provide online courses and degree programs.	5	4	3	2	1
2. Partner with state universities to offer baccalaureate level courses on the college campus.	5	4	3	2	1
3. Incorporating service learning across the college curriculum.	5	4	3	2	1
4. Pursuing enrollment growth initiatives to increase enrollment 20% by 2005.	5	4	3	2	1
5. Pursuing specialized accreditation or certification for eligible programs.	5	4	3	2	1

The Board Planning Session: Engaging the Board, Administration, Faculty, and Staff into the Planning Process

The annual board planning session is a critical component of successful, ongoing planning efforts. This annual session allows the board, administration, and selected members of faculty and staff to determine priorities of the college for the next three to five years. Goals are established to address issues of concern and key opportunities for the institution to attain its mission and achieve its vision.

Several benefits are derived from the annual board planning session including:

- allowing board members, administrators and key faculty and staff to review and understand basic and preliminary planning information and data;

- providing an opportunity to clearly communicate the value of planning throughout the institution;

- establishing clear directives to articulate the institution's response to current challenges and prescribing actions necessary to achieve desired outcomes;

- providing a forum for healthy dialog among members of the board, administration, faculty and staff;

- establishing an environment that allows planning to occur with stakeholder input, rather than top-down administrative initiative.

Establishing the Annual Board Planning Session Agenda

Two fundamental tools facilitate preparation for the board planning session — the environmental scan and the Board Planning Survey. The environmental scan provides preliminary information on key trends, issues, and challenges facing the institution. The Board Planning Survey highlights these issues and challenges and assesses the board members' priorities for the institution. In combination, these two instruments provide the basis for a productive board planning effort. Exhibits 4-9 and 4-10, discussed in detail later in this chapter, provide a planning flowchart and a suggested timeline to apply these and other planning tools.

Prior to the annual board planning session, significant preparatory work must be done by the president, administration, faculty and staff. An agenda needs to be developed based on the Board Planning Survey responses. Results of the environmental scan should be highlighted for each major division in the college. All of these components are brought together several months prior to the actual board planning session.

The agenda is developed during regular key administrator meetings, chaired by the president, with the vice-presidents, deans or directors articulating challenges, issues, and desired goals from their respective areas. Initial items that should be reflected in the agenda include a review of the current college mission and vision statement, overview of the results of the environmental scan, Board Planning Survey responses, and briefings from each vice-president or dean on key issues and recommended goals. All of the agenda items should be thoroughly discussed in meetings prior to establishing the final agenda. This ensures that the administration is cohesive regarding its goals and recommendations.

The agenda should identify each major topic, with established time limits for presentations and discussion. A designated presenter for each topic facilitates initial preparation for the planning session and ensures that all stakeholders focus on the agenda item at hand, without straying into discussions that are not pertinent. A sample board planning session agenda is shown at Exhibit 4-4.

EXHIBIT 4-4

BOARD PLANNING SESSION-SAMPLE AGENDA

1. Review mission and vision statement. *President – 10 min.*

2. Discuss results of environmental scan data. *President and Administration – 60 min.*

3. Discuss results of Board Planning Survey – identify and prioritize institutional challenges and desired outcomes. *President and Board members – 15 min.*

4. Develop and refine institutional goals to reflect and achieve the Board's priorities. *President, Board – 60 min.*

5. Briefings from each major division and proposed goals for 2003-2008.

   a. Student Services - *V.P. Student Services – 30 min.*

   b. Finance and Operations- *V.P. Fin. & Operation – 30 min.*

   c. Planning and Development – *Dir. Planning & Dev. – 30 min.*

   d. Instruction- *V.P. of Instruction-30 min.*

   e. Intercollegiate athletics – *Dir. of Athletics – 30 min.*

6. Review of current financial status of college. *V.P. Finance & Operations – 30 min.*

7. FY 200X revenue projections by revenue sources based on most current projections. *V.P. Finance & Operations – 15 min.*

8. FY 200X budget expenditures by functional area. *V.P.'s, president – 60 min.*

   a. Ideal budget based on current plans and projected growth.

   b. Proposed budget based on FY 200X actual expenditures/projected growth.

   c. Balanced budget as required by Board Policy.

9. Impact on 7b and c. (Executive Session to discuss personnel matters required.)

10. Open discussion to determine Board guidance. *President, V.P.'s – 60 min.*

The agenda should be organized to help the board make decisions that determine the future of the college. In some cases, an executive session may need to be conducted to discuss such things as personnel issues before proceeding with the meeting. The authors strongly encourage action on discussion items to take place at the next regular board meeting. This allows the president and administration time to prepare items for official action. It also provides the board another opportunity to review the outcomes of their discussions before finalizing items that require official board action, e.g. change in mission, vision, institutional goals.

Developing the Planning Document

After the board planning session is completed, the institution is ready to begin developing the written plan. The president's office, the director of planning or another designated individual should be assigned to consistently coordinate the process and develop the planning document.

The primary components of a mid-range plan are listed below. Generally, one to two pages are adequate to address each of the components with the exception of the division goals, capital projects and the equipment plans. These items, along with a brief explanation and example for each one, are provided to aid in formatting the planning document.

- Mission Statement – The plan should contain the most current version of the institution's mission statement. Any changes recommended and approved by the board in the planning session should be included.

- Vision Statement – The most current version of the vision statement should be included.

- Board's Institutional Goals – These goals are established and approved by the board as a result of the planning session. See Exhibit 4-5 on page 56 for sample institutional goals.

- Planning parameters – Planning parameters are often developed as a result of the institution's environmental scan. A brief section identifying the results of the scan and the impact they will have on the institution for the planning period, help to establish the scope for planning. Sample parameters might include: 1) Use projected 2002-03 enrollment, which is three percent higher than 2001-02; 2) Assessed valuation will increase to $78 million; 3) The mill levy will increase to 40 mills; 4) The division between academic and vocational enrollment percentages will be 60-40.

- Planning guidelines — Planning guidelines describe how various components of the planning process will be conducted. Examples of planning guidelines include: 1) Budget targets will be based on the board of trustees approved budget for the current fiscal year, enrollment growth experienced during the past fiscal year, and the current budget deficit; 2) Budget line items that will be centrally controlled are a) salaries and benefits, b) adjunct salaries, and c) special pay; 3) Dollars allocated in budget line items, other than those mentioned in paragraph two above, may be transferred from one budget category to another as necessary to achieve budgeting goals and maximum flexibility; and 4) A budget review will occur twice a year (October 1 and February 1) for the year 2002-03 school year.

EXHIBIT 4-5

The Board of Trustees at its April 13, 2003 meeting, reviewed its institutional objectives for the period of July 1, 2002- June 30, 2007. After considerable discussion, the Board agreed to focus college resources to ensure:

- *Continued accreditation for the maximum duration allowed under The Higher Learning Commission of North Central Association guidelines.*
- *Continued enrollment growth.*
- *Meeting the higher education needs of students and the community.*
- *Continued professional development of the Board of Trustees and college employees.*

INSTITUTIONAL GOALS

1. Seek NCA/HLC accreditation for the maximum duration.
2. Direct college efforts and initiatives to ensure continued enrollment growth.
   a. Maintain a rate of enrollment growth that equals or exceeds the average annual increase among Kansas community colleges.
   b. Increase enrollment to 1,000 FTE by June 30, 2005.
   c. Strengthen target marketing and recruitment efforts to ensure continued enrollment growth.
   d. Develop strategies to ensure high student retention.
   e. Expand college infrastructure to meet the increased student population.
   f. Develop and maintain a philosophy throughout the college of meeting and adapting to community needs throughout the growth process.
3. Ensure the higher education needs of students and the community are being met.
4. Provide professional development opportunities for the Board of Trustees and college employees.
5. Demonstrate the overall improvement of student learning across the institution.

- Organizational chart and structure – A brief section that includes a current organizational chart and an explanation of the roles and responsibilities of the president, vice-presidents, and directors is valuable.

- Division goals, objectives and strategies – A separate section for the goals, objectives and strategies for each major division of the college should be established. Typical functional areas would include student services, instruction, finance and operations, and athletics. The goal page includes the goals, objectives and strategies, target dates, implementation and annual costs, account number, office of responsibility and a column devoted to cross-referencing. The account number and cross-referencing columns are discussed in more detail in Chapter 5. These two columns link the goals and objectives to other college processes. See Exhibit 4-6 on page 58 for a sample goal page from the student services division.

- Equipment Plans – These will be discussed in more detail in Chapter 5. A discussion of how they are developed and sample equipment plans will be included.

- Other – Additional items may be added in the appendices. These items include a brief overview of the planning process, self-study process schedule, capital projects list, budget information, and other information institution leaders feel strengthen the plan.

EXHIBIT 4-6

Mid-Range Plan, 2002-2007
Division: Student Services

Goals & Objectives	Target Date	Implementation/ Annual Costs	Account Number	Office of Responsibility	Cross-Reference
Goal #1 Increase student support services and course offerings to outlying communities and high schools in the service area, including use of alternative modes of delivery that are tailored to meet student demands and needs for course offerings	May 2007	$25,000	11-1462 11-1463 11-1464	V.P. Student Services V.P. of Inst. Outreach Directors	See *2001-2006 MRP,* pg. 76
a. Increase credit hour production to support institutional goal.	July 2004				
i. Incorporate recruiting strategies established by the institution to ensure enrollment growth.	Sept. 2005	$25,000			
ii. Work to secure adequate enrollment in classes to prevent cancellation of courses and associated negative repercussions.	Aug. 2006	$ 5,500			

Communicating the Plan

Once the plan is complete, it is critical to communicate it effectively to internal and external institutional audiences. Communication to external audiences builds support and credibility. More importantly, communicating the plan to internal audiences—the board, administration, faculty, and staff — creates ownership, support, credibility, accountability, and an expectation of implementation and follow through.

Keys to ensuring that the plan will be used are: 1) continually engage and educate the board of trustees on the planning process; 2) establish a procedure of reporting and evaluating that allows the board to hold the president and administration accountable for the achievement of the goals outlined in the plan; 3) establish an administrative evaluative procedure that ensures staff and faculty consistently pursue the plan's objectives; 5) distribute the plan to key stakeholders in the institution; and 6) continually reference the plan in board, division, and departmental meetings to ensure activities continue to support the goals.

The first step in this process, continually educating and engaging the board of trustees in planning, was detailed in Chapter 2. Once the plan is completed, it should be presented to the board for approval or endorsement. Each board member should receive a copy of the plan and once it's approved, the president needs to keep the goals outlined in the plan at the forefront of college activities. A briefing by the board chair and the president to the faculty and staff at the fall semester inservice meeting is an excellent way to establish the direction for the upcoming year and communicate the institution's commitment to the planning process. Any changes to the mission or vision statement should be addressed, along with an overview of the board's institutional goals. In subsequent meetings, each vice-president, dean or director should brief their faculty and staff on division goals that will be addressed in the upcoming year. During the division meetings, a copy of the completed plan should be distributed to all deans, directors, faculty and key staff members. A summary of the institutional mission statement and goals should be displayed in appropriate faculty and staff work areas.

Establishing and Utilizing Planning Sessions at Every Level of the Institution

Once the plan has been approved by the board of trustees and employees have been briefed on its contents, the administration must begin leading the institution into activities or strategies directed at attaining the goals. Monitoring progress and tracking achievement are critical to making the planning process work. Mechanisms to aid the institution with these processes will be discussed in more detail in Chapter 6.

Approximately six months after the initial implementation of the plan, it is time to begin conducting planning retreats with faculty and staff representing the major divisions and departments within the institution. Separate retreats should be organized for faculty representatives and staff personnel. Department chairs represent the instructional division at the faculty retreat session. Key staff from the major functional areas of the college, e.g. Student Services, Athletics, Development and Finance and Operations comprise the institutional representatives for the staff planning retreat. The president and key administrators should attend both retreats to provide information, direction and facilitation.

Retreats for both groups should be designed so planning outcomes align with the college mission, vision and institutional goals. These meetings are an important part of the preparation for the board planning session because they provide an opportunity for faculty and staff to provide input into existing goals and develop new goals which will address current division and college issues and challenges. They will often be the best sources of information about opportunities for growth or improvement that exist in the institution's environment.

A brief agenda (Exhibit 4-7) should be developed and communicated to all individuals who will be involved in the planning retreats. Faculty and staff should be prepared to provide input on suggested goal areas they feel should be incorporated into the plan. A sample agenda for the faculty and administrative retreat is shown on the following page.

EXHIBIT 4-7

Faculty and Administration Planning Retreat Agenda

- *Review current mission and vision statement. President – 15 min.*

- *Review progress on current institutional goals. President – 30 min.*

- *Review results of Board Planning Session survey. President – 15 min.*

- *Discuss estimated 2003-04 Budget- a) Overall college budget, b) Instructional division budget, and c) Instructional support budget. President and V.P. Instruction – 30 min.*

- *Discuss current external and internal constraints for the division. V. P. Instruction – 30 min.*

- *Review progress of Instructional Division goals from previous year. V. P. Instruction – 30 min.*

- *Develop goals with estimated target dates, implementation costs and offices of responsibility. V. P. Instruction and Faculty – 120 min.*

- *Open discussion- V.P. Instruction, president and faculty – 60 min.*

A similar format, focusing on all aspects of the institution, can be used to develop the staff and administration planning agenda. The final outcomes of the planning retreats should include a review of the mission and vision statements, discussion of constraints facing the divisions and departments, and new goals to address current issues and challenges. Sample goals and objectives generated as a result of the faculty and staff planning retreats are provided in Exhibit 4-8.

EXHIBIT 4-8

OUTCOMES OF FACULTY RETREAT

Goal: Improve the student learning outcomes of the developmental studies program.

Objective #1 – Implement an intensive academic development program designed for students whose entering basic skills are substantially below standard.

Objective #2 – Utilize outcomes data to target instructional enhancements to increase student success in developmental courses.

OUTCOMES OF STAFF RETREAT

Student Services – Goal: Provide a residence hall environment that meets students' needs including safety, security, self development, learning and social interaction.

Objective #1 – Develop programming opportunities for residence hall students to include social, educational and community activities.

Finance and Operations – Goal: Provide capital improvements for all facilities necessary to attract and retain students and improve internal plant operations.

Objective # 1– Complete the following planned projects for 2003-04. 1) Replace carpet in the main classroom building, 2) Install a sprinkler system in the main classroom building, 3) Install a student snack bar in the student commons area, and 4) Renovate residence hall suites and common areas in two of the four dorms.

After goals and objectives have been established, target dates and estimated costs of implementation should be determined. Offices of responsibility should be identified to determine accountability for overseeing the implementation of activities. When the planning retreats are completed, the vice-president, dean or director is then ready to present the updated goals and new goals at the board planning session.

EXHIBIT 4-9

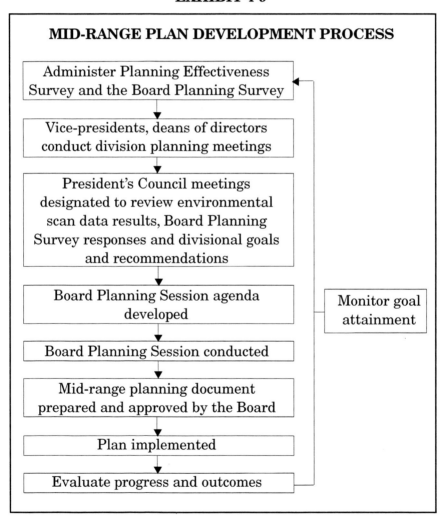

MID-RANGE PLAN DEVELOPMENT PROCESS

Administer Planning Effectiveness Survey and the Board Planning Survey

Vice-presidents, deans of directors conduct division planning meetings

President's Council meetings designated to review environmental scan data results, Board Planning Survey responses and divisional goals and recommendations

Board Planning Session agenda developed

Monitor goal attainment

Board Planning Session conducted

Mid-range planning document prepared and approved by the Board

Plan implemented

Evaluate progress and outcomes

EXHIBIT 4-10

SUGGESTED PLANNING CALENDAR

DECEMBER
- Environmental scan completed and results reviewed and compiled.
- President sends directive to deans, directors and vice-presidents to begin the planning necessary to conduct faculty and staff planning retreats.
- Planning Effectiveness Survey administered and results addressed.

JANUARY
- Faculty and staff planning retreat agendas prepared by presidents, vice president, deans, and directors.
- Faculty and staff planning retreats conducted.
- Board Planning Session survey administered and results compiled.

FEBRUARY
- Each dean, director and vice-president presents briefing of recommended revised goals and new goals (from faculty and staff planning retreat input) to be approved or modified by the administration and presented at a series of President's Council meetings.
- Planning guidelines and parameters are established.
- Administration communicates with faculty and staff regarding the administration's changes and approvals of goals and objectives.

MARCH/APRIL
- The board planning session is conducted.

MAY-JULY
- Draft planning document is prepared.

AUGUST
- Planning document is presented to the Board for approval.

SEPTEMBER-FEBRUARY
- Initiatives underway to attain goals identified in the planning document.

The Planning Cycle

The entire planning cycle has now been discussed. The faculty and staff retreats, along with the work of the vice-presidents, deans and directors, establishes the foundation necessary for the board planning session. Exhibit 4-9 illustrates the complete planning cycle. Exhibit 4-10 presents a sample timeline that the institution may use to ensure that each component is incorporated and the planning process is completed and becomes a fully integrated aspect of the operation.

The institution will reap tremendous benefits by implementing a planning process that is incorporated into its ongoing daily operations. However, the planning process should not stand alone. In order to be truly effective, the planning process must be linked to budgeting, outcomes assessment and facilities and equipment planning. Chapter 5 will identify ways to help institutions expand the planning process so that it can be linked to these important functions.

Summary

Establishing the mid-range planning process ensures that the institution will incorporate the various facets of planning into their daily operations. Before the process can be established or streamlined to be more effective, the implementation of a planning survey will help identify strengths and weaknesses with current processes. Establishing the board planning agenda is critical to the success of the annual planning session. This annual session provides an excellent forum for the board, administration, faculty and staff to identify key issues and challenges that need to be addressed in order to make decisions affecting the future direction of the college. The outcome of the planning session provides the framework for the revised plan, and it is important that it is referenced and used in regular board, staff and faculty meetings to establish institutional activities necessary to support the goals and objectives identified in the plan. The mid-range planning process, once implemented, will establish the environment that is necessary to attain institutional goals.

FOOTNOTES

1. Covey, Steven, *The 7 Habits of Highly Effective People — Powerful Lessons in Personal Change.* Simon & Schuster, 1989. pg. 99.

2. Roalman, A. "Why Corporations Hate the Future", *MBA,* 9, (1975), pg. 36.

5

What Makes It Work ... Linking Planning to Budgeting, Facilities and Equipment Management, and the Outcomes Assessment Process

- Linking planning to the institutional budgeting process

- Linking planning to facilities and equipment management

- Linking the planning and outcomes assessment processes

- Incorporating institutional standing committee recommendations into the planning process

- Expanding the planning cycle calendar

The Importance of Linking Planning to Budgeting, Facilities and Equipment Management, and Outcomes Assessment Processes

Chapter 4 provided a detailed overview of how to implement the planning process and develop the planning document. Institutions that foster clear planning processes resulting in well-organized written plans are positioned for effective planning. However, if planning is to be ongoing and continuous, it must be linked to other primary functions of the institution — namely, budgeting, facilities and equipment management, and outcomes assessment processes. Without a mechanism to link these important processes, planning fails to drive other major key institutional functions.

Regional and specialized accrediting associations review planning processes at their member institutions during team visits and determine whether the planning process has been incorporated into the "fabric" of the institution. By studying planning and budgeting documents, accreditation teams examine an institution's commitment to improving its educational programs and effectively utilizing its resources. Further, these documents provide evidence of the institution's awareness of issues and challenges that need to be addressed to improve its operations and better achieve its stated mission.

It is important to bear in mind that the processes described in this chapter cannot be implemented within one year. Each major component prescribed in this chapter must be phased in as planning and operations processes progress and are refined.

Linking the Planning Process to Budgeting

One of the most crucial and sometimes baffling institutional challenges is linking planning with the budgeting process. This particular linkage often confounds leaders as they strive to align these two processes. This section will focus on three primary avenues for the institution to establish this important linkage.

Incorporate Costs and Account Numbers on Goal Pages Within the Plan

One of the primary ways to link planning to the budget process is to incorporate and align estimated costs with accompanying account numbers into the goal pages established for each division in the plan. (See Exhibit 4-6, Chapter 4.) These costs will be used later in the process as budget priorities are developed and established during the budget workshops.

Establish Planning Guidelines for Budget Development

Planning guidelines were defined and discussed in Chapter 4. After reviewing environmental scan data results, the institution should be able to establish planning guidelines. These guidelines help to direct the overall planning and budgeting process. Factors such as projected enrollment and revenue figures, budget review frequency, and budget line item transfer procedures comprise appropriate guidelines. These guidelines ensure that the administration and staff adhere to consistent planning and budget development.

Establishing the guidelines early in the planning process enables the administration and staff to estimate costs for individual and aggregate goals. Although the budget will not yet be finalized during early stages of the planning process, the chief financial officer should be able to provide each major division with estimated revenue availability. These amounts are based on projections of the mill levy, assessed property valuation, state and county out-district tuition, state aid rates, and other sources of funding. As the planning and attendant budgeting process evolves, adjustments may need to be made based on actual dollar amounts.

Using Budget Workshops

To effectively address the financial feasibility of attaining planned goals, institution leaders may find it beneficial to conduct a series of budget workshops with the board of trustees approximately two months before the budget is to be finalized. These workshops provide the board and administration the opportunity to review the goals and objectives outlined in the plan, analyze associated costs, and determine funding options to support the goals targeted for the year.

The budget workshops should be designed so that each vice-president or dean provides the board a briefing on goals and objectives, estimated costs and projected target dates for their division. In addition, the vice-presidents or deans should present the financial impact that their goals will have on the division and the institution.

In each budget planning workshop, the Board and the administration need to work together to determine: 1) Do individual division goals support the institutional goals? 2) What financial impact do the goals have on the division and the institution? 3) What additional personnel, equipment, facilities, etc., will be necessary to attain and support the goal? 4) Is it financially feasible to attain the goals during the time frame suggested?

When presentations by the vice–presidents or deans have been completed, the board and administration establish goal priorities. If the board and administration determine that a particular goal is a high priority, but revenues are insufficient to fund it during the current fiscal period, they may choose to extend the target date or seek other funding sources. If they choose to fund the goal in the absence of additional resources, institution leaders now have three options: 1) Rearrange existing funds; 2) Utilize monies from the cash reserve to supplement funding; or 3) Include the item as part of the package that needs new funding which would require an increase in the local mill levy or other funding sources. To illustrate this process, the following goal from the Finance and Operations division is used.

EXHIBIT 5-1

GOAL: Provide capital improvements for all facilities necessary to attract and retain students and to improve internal plant operations.

- **Total budget for capital improvements for 2003-04 — $165,000**

- **Total estimated cost for prioritized capital projects for 2003-04 — $200,000**

- **Difference — ($35,000)**

The funding options that are available:

1) *The $35,000 difference can be moved from the Instruction, Student Services, Athletics and Finance and Operations divisions, with each administrator identifying approximately $9,000 to surrender to fund the capital project priorities.*

Impact: Delay of certain goals targeted for 2003-04 in each major division. Reduction in some services and programs.

2) *Withdraw $35,000 from the cash reserve. The current cash reserve is at $975,000. It is currently below the Board's desired level of $1 million dollars. By withdrawing $35,000, this would reduce the cash reserve to $940,000.*

Impact: Dwindling cash reserve. Increase in the local mill levy. Because the local mill levy is already high for the county, the board chose not to exercise this option for the $35,000 deficit.

The Board and Administration selected option one — rearrange existing funds to pay for prioritized capital projects.

The planning process extends into the budget development phase as the goals and anticipated costs are reviewed and funding alternatives are identified. The proposed budget calendar shown in Exhibit 5-2 links the institutional planning process to the budget development process.

EXHIBIT 5-2

SAMPLE BUDGET CALENDAR
2003-2004

May 20, 2003 ....Division Budgets to Vice Presidents and President

June 7, 2003 ....Budgets to Vice President of Finance

June 17, 2002 ....Tentative Budget Ready

June 19, 2003 ....Budget document completed

June 24, 2003 ....Regular Board Meeting and Instructional Division Budget Review

*July 1, 2003 ....Budget presentations by Development, Student Services, Office of the President, and Athletics (Additional Board meeting)

*July 15, 2003 ......Regular Board meeting with Finance & Operations; Budget Wrap Up; Agreement to publish budget

August 2, 2003 .....Advertise Budget (Notice of Hearing)

August 12, 2003 ...Regular Board Meeting and public hearing of final legal budget. Vote to adopt or modify budget.

August 22, 2003 ...File Budget with County Clerk and Board of Regents

Linking the Planning Process to
Facilities and Equipment Management

Developing a consistent link between planning and budget development may take two or more years. Only when planning and budgeting are well connected, is the institution ready to move forward to integrate facilities and equipment management with the planning process.

Two major practices guide the institution on effectively joining facilities and equipment management to ongoing institutional planning. These include: 1) establishing a facilities committee; and 2) developing departmental and division equipment plans.

Establishing a Facilities Committee

One of the first tasks that the institution can undertake to merge facilities and equipment management is to establish a Facilities Committee. This committee should be comprised of the chief financial administrator, the director of facilities and maintenance, and representatives from faculty and staff. The primary purpose of the committee is to review and prioritize facility and equipment requests and to prepare a prioritized recommendation on capital projects. This recommendation is developed on an annual basis and is discussed at the annual Board planning and subsequent budget sessions. A sample capital projects list is shown in Exhibit 5-3.

In addition to the capital projects list, it is beneficial for planning purposes for the Facilities Committee to continue to list and track completion of all capital improvements for the five-year planning period. A simple table showing the project, year of anticipated completion, estimated and actual costs is a simple and beneficial way for the institution to systematically track capital projects. In the event that the institution receives increased funding to support additional capital projects, it provides a way to quickly identify projects and establish their priority based on additional revenue sources. This table should be made available to the board at the annual planning session and included in the final plan. See Exhibit 5-4 for a partial sample five-year capital budget.

EXHIBIT 5-3

CAPITAL PROJECTS
2003-04

PROJECT	BUDGET

1. Recarpet Student Conference Center ....$ 16,000

2. Upgrade emergency notification system ....$ 13,000

3. Remodel restroom in main classroom building ...$ 12,000

4. Install automatic doors in the Student
   Conference Center ....$ 22,000

5. Install permanent snack bar in the main
   classroom building ....$ 15,000

6. Remodel personnel office area. ....$ 15,000

7. Remodel classroom #3 in the main
   classsroom building. ....$ 3,000

2003-04 Capital Outlay Budget ....**$ 96,000**

If additional revenue is available, this
additional project will be completed.

8. Remodel for a One Stop Center in the
   main classroom building. ....$ 70,000

TOTAL *$166,000*

EXHIBIT 5-4

PROJECT	2002-03	2003-04	2004-05	2005-06	2006-2007	Project Total	Actual Cost Completed
Renovate instructional building	$25,000					$ 25,000	
Construct storm shelter for power line building				$30,000		$ 30,000	
Remodel Room #3	$ 3,000					$ 3,000	
Replace air handling unit	$ 20,000					$ 20,000	
Recarpet Student Conf. Center	$ 16,000					$ 16,000	
Upgrade emergency notif. system	$ 13,000				·	$ 13,000	
Remodel restrooms in main classroom building	$ 12,000	$ 12,000	$12,000	$ 12,000	$ 12,000	$ 60,000	
Install automatic doors in SCC	$ 11,000	$ 11,000				$ 22,000	
Remodel personnel office area	$ 15,000					$ 15,000	
Remodel for One Stop Center	$ 70,000	$ 70,000				$140,000	
Remodel SCC basement				$ 40,000	$ 50,000	$ 90,000	
Install snack bar	$ 15,000	$ 35,000				$ 50,000	
Install new scoreboard			$20,000	$ 20,000		$ 40,000	
Install technology upgrades				$ 50,000	$ 50,000	$100,000	
Construct storage facility					$ 25,000	$ 25,000	
TOTAL	$200,000	$128,000	$32,000	$152,000	$137,000	$649,000	

Division and Departmental Equipment Plans

The development of annual equipment plans provides another mechanism to help institutions identify current and future equipment needs. Prior to the annual budget workshops, each instructional department and every major division (i.e. Student Services, Athletics, Finance and Operations, etc.) prepares a five–year prioritized equipment plan. This plan aids the chief administrator in determining funds necessary to support equipment needs. During the budget workshops, equipment priorities are incorporated into each major division's presentation and the necessary funding is identified.

A simple form is completed and updated annually by each instructional department and the chief administrator of the division. It is important to allow flexibility for unforeseen equipment replacement needs. A sample instructional department equipment plan is shown in Exhibit 5-5 and a division equipment plan is shown in Exhibit 5-6.

EXHIBIT 5-5

SAMPLE INSTRUCTIONAL DEPARTMENT EQUIPMENT PLAN

BUSINESS AND ACCOUNTING DEPARTMENT
FIVE-YEAR EQUIPMENT PLAN
2003-2008

Program and Equipment Description	Cost Each	Total Cost	Replacement (R) New (N)	Projected Year of Purchase
Acctg.				
(23) Computers	$ 1,800	$41,400	R	2003-04
(5) Calculators	$ 140	$ 700	R	2003-04
Bus.				
(5) Transcribing Machines	$ 650	$ 3,250	R	2003-04
(1) Laser color printer	$ 500	$ 500	R	2003-04
Bus. & Acc.				
(2) Laser printers	$ 3,000	$ 6,000	R	2003-04
TOTAL FOR 2003-04		**$51,800**		
Bus.				
(23) Computers	$ 1,800	$41,400	R	2004-05
(5) Calculators	$ 140	$ 700	R	2004-05
(5) Transcribers	$ 650	$ 3,250	R	2004-05
(5) Docking stations	$ 600	$ 3,000	R	2004-05
TOTAL for 2004-05		**$48,350**		
Acctg.				
(23) Computers	$ 1,800	$41,400	R	2005-06
(5) Calculators	$ 140	$ 700	R	2005-06
Bus.				
(5) Transcribers	$ 650	$ 3,250	R	2005-06
TOTAL FOR 2005-06		**$45,350**		
Bus.				
(23) Computers	$ 1,800	$41,400	R	2006-07
(5) Calculators	$ 140	$ 700	R	2006-07
(5) Transcribers	$ 650	$ 3,250	R	2006-07
TOTAL FOR 2006-07		**$45,350**		
Acctg.				
(23) Computers	$ 1,800	$41,400	R	2007-08
(5) Calculators	$ 140	$ 700	R	2007-08
Bus.				
(5) Transcribers	$ 650	$ 3,250	R	2007-08
TOTAL FOR 2007-08		**$45,350**		
TOTAL FOR BUSINESS AND ACCTG.		**$236,200**		

EXHIBIT 5-6

SAMPLE DIVISION EQUIPMENT PLAN

ATHLETIC DEPARTMENT
FIVE-YEAR EQUIPMENT PLAN
2003-2008

Program and Equipment Description	Cost Each	Total Cost	Replacement (R) New (N)	Projected Year of Purchase
Baseball Roll away hitting cage	$ 4,000	$ 4,000	R	2003-04
Women's basketball Computer	$ 1,500	$ 1,500	N	2003-04
Basketball Shot clocks	$ 5,000	$ 5,000	R	2003-04
Volleyball Computer Volleyball Standards	$ 1,500 $ 4,000	$ 1,500 $ 4,000	N R	2003-04 2003-04
Athletic Office Laptop computer	$ 2,400	$ 2,400	N	2003-04
Softball Pitching machine	$ 2,000	$ 2,000	N	2003-04
TOTAL FOR 2003-04		**$20,400**		
Baseball Gator	$ 5,000	$ 5,000	N	2004-05
TOTAL for 2005-06		**$ 5,000**		
Athletics Public address system	$15,000	$15,000	R	2005-06
TOTAL FOR 2005-06		**$15,000**		
Baseball Drag/leveler/broom	$ 4,000	$ 4,000	N	2006-07
TOTAL FOR 2006-07		**$ 4,000**		
Basketball Scoreboard	$50,000	$50,000	R	2007-08
TOTAL FOR 2007-08		**$50,000**		
TOTAL FOR ATHLETICS		*$94,400*		

Linking the Planning and Outcomes Assessment Processes

Outcomes assessment is a critical process taking place in every educational institution across the country. Renewed focus on graduating students' knowledge and skills, caught public attention and caused regional and specialized accreditation organizations to adjust their standards to ensure that adequate assessment processes are in place. These processes answer questions about student learning and the effectiveness of an institution's operations. Assessment is becoming increasingly significant in the institution's daily operations and needs to be addressed in the overall planning process.

This section will identify three ways that an institution can associate mid-range planning and assessment processes.

Ensure That a Solid Outcomes Assessment Plan Is in Place

Before the institutional planning and assessment processes can be connected, it is important that the institution has a comprehensive outcomes assessment plan in place. This plan should clearly identify goals and objectives for assessment of the instructional functions and outline initiatives to enhance institutional effectiveness. It is common for some goals of the outcomes plan to pertain to specific individual instructional or operational departments, while others impact numerous functions of the institution. Goals that have an impact on the institution should be brought forth and incorporated into the mid-range plan. This ensures goals that merit institutional-wide support are clearly communicated to all affected departments and divisions.

To illustrate this point, assume that the following goal is included in the institution's outcomes assessment plan: "Implement an entering examination to determine students' readiness to enroll in college level courses." This particular goal should be incorporated into the Instructional Division section of the mid-range plan for the following reasons: 1) the cost of implementation of this testing program will probably require additional institutional funds; 2) the Counseling or Testing Office needs to be involved in the process to determine testing and placement procedures; 3) the Admissions Office needs to be aware of entry testing requirements in order to effectively inform students and adjust printed recruiting materials; 4) the Instructional Division will select the test, determine placement cut-off scores, and identify or develop appro-

78

priate classes for student placement; 5) the Finance and Operations division needs to be aware of the goal to anticipate additional funding requirements.

As the outcomes assessment plan is reviewed and revised annually (ideally late spring), goals considered for incorporation into the mid-range plan should be highlighted at the board planning session. This should be based on a recommendation from the Outcomes Assessment Committee or the chief academic officer.

Incorporating Program and Functional Area Review Recommendations

One of the primary assessment tools used in the instructional area, and increasingly in other functional areas of the institution, is the program review process. The program review historically has been utilized in the instructional area to monitor faculty credentials, enrollment trend data, budget and expenditures, and other key elements that help identify strengths and weaknesses of the program or department. Many institutions are now utilizing a similar process to review functional areas such as Financial Aid, Student Services, Testing and Counseling, Admissions and other important areas in the college to determine their effectiveness. These functional area reviews should identify weaknesses and challenges that need to be addressed by the department or program, along with a set of recommendations to address concerns and improve overall effectiveness. Recommendations that arise from these reviews often need the support of the entire institution. As a result, goals to address these recommendations should be included in the planning process. As the program reviews are completed in late spring, the chief academic officer or the administrator of the functional area, should submit proposed goals to be discussed at the board planning session.

This process offers two primary advantages: 1) it ensures that the recommendations from the reviews are identified and incorporated into the planning process; and 2) it provides a means of ensuring that the reviews are utilized in a manner that will benefit the program, department, or institution.

Linking the Planning Process
to Standing Committee Recommendations

The standing committee structure is vital to any college. These diverse groups address current and ongoing issues and concerns within the institution. Generally, committees are comprised of faculty, staff, administration, and students with a related interest or expertise in the topic to be addressed. Each committee provides recommendations to address issues identified in its charge or assigned by the administration.

An important part of the planning process is the review of committee recommendations. During the later part of the planning cycle (generally late spring) each committee should be tasked to provide a brief annual activity report that includes recommendations resulting from their discussions. These reports should be submitted to the president and executive administration to determine: 1) if the recommendation merits institutional attention; 2) if the recommendations should be incorporated into the goals and objectives of the functional areas outlined in the plan; 3) if the recommendation can be addressed by a single office or department; or 4) if the recommendation should be addressed in another manner.

If the recommendation should be incorporated into the goals and objectives of a particular functional area of the institution, the president should task the chief administrator overseeing the area to develop a goal (or utilize the committee's recommendation) to be incorporated into the goals for that area. A recommendation that merits institutional attention by the board and president may need to be written in goal form and presented for the board's consideration at the planning session. Others that merit attention by a single office or department should be tasked by the president or chief administrator to address the issue.

The benefits of utilizing recommendations that come forth from the standing committees are: 1) committee members feel that their recommendations are taken seriously and will be addressed; 2) the institution benefits from solid recommendations that can help improve its programs and services; and 3) it continues to engage employees in the decision-making and planning processes of the institution.

Utilizing the Cross-Reference Column to Highlight Key Budgeting, Outcomes Assessment and Facilities and Equipment Support Documents

In Chapter 4, a detailed goal page form from the mid-range plan is shown as Exhibit 4-6. The form includes columns for goals and objectives, target date, implementation or annual costs, account number, office of responsibility and cross-references. The cross-reference plays an important role in providing an additional means to link planning with budgeting, outcomes assessment, facilities and equipment management.

Goals outlined in the plan that directly support assessment efforts should include a citation in the cross-reference column that shows the assessment plan version and associated page number. Those identified in the Finance and Operations section should have citations that link goals to recommendations from the Facilities Committee or the capital projects list. Both the Facilities Committee report and the capital projects list should be appended to the mid-range plan.

This simple process involves little time, but provides another means to ensure that budgeting, assessment, facilities and equipment management are supported in the institution's mid-range plan.

The Expanded Planning Calendar

As a result of the additional work necessary to merge planning with budgeting, outcomes assessment, facilities and equipment management, the planning calendar must be expanded to reflect these additions. An expanded planning calendar, incorporating the linkages discussed in this chapter are italicized and show on the following page as Exhibit 5-7.

EXHIBIT 5-7

SUGGESTED EXPANDED PLANNING CALENDAR

December – President sends directive to deans, directors and vice-presidents to begin the preparation necessary for the faculty, staff and Board planning sessions.

January – Faculty and staff planning retreats conducted.

February – Each dean, director and vice-president presents briefing of revised goals and new goals to be presented to the Board at a series of President's Council meetings. Planning guidelines and parameters are established.

March – Standing committee recommendations submitted to president and incorporated into the Board Planning Session agenda where appropriate.

- *Capital projects priority list and budget submitted to president and incorporated in the Board Planning Session agenda.*

- *Outcomes assessment goals to be incorporated into the mid-range plan submitted to the President and incorporated into the Board Planning Session agenda.*

- *Program review recommendations submitted to chief academic officer and chief administrator of the functional area reviewed.*

- *Board Planning Session agenda finalized.*

April – The Board Planning Session is conducted.

May – *Division and departmental equipment plans submitted.*

June-July – *Budget workshops conducted and final budget prepared.*
Planning document prepared.

August – Planning document is presented to the Board for approval.

September-February – Initiatives are underway to attain goals identified in the planning document.

Summary

As noted throughout this chapter, planning cannot occur in isolation from the budgeting process. Successful, usable plans result from linking together facilities management, supplies and equipment, staffing, etc., as a first step. The plan takes on more meaning when the entire college is somehow involved. The college's committee structure, if used properly, provides for that involvement. The final link, i.e., to the outcomes assessment process, gives meaning to the term "comprehensive planning."

6

Keep It Going ... Ensuring that the Mid-Range Planning Process Stays

- Developing a board policy that incorporates the planning function into board responsibilities

- Utilizing a quarterly reporting process to monitor progress toward goals and establish accountability

- Implementing an annual review process of the mid-range plan

Many institutions expend significant time and effort on board planning sessions and preparing written planning documents, but they often fail to establish mechanisms that ensure accountability and continuity. Many well-written plans are shelved, leaving institutions scrambling for an integrated process when an accreditation visit approaches.

This chapter presents three primary tools to assist institutions in building accountability for achieving plan goals and monitoring the planning process to ensure that it continues. Three key issues are addressed: 1) establishing a board policy supporting the planning function; 2) utilizing quarterly reports to provide updates on goal attainment; and 3) establishing an annual process to review the mid-range plan.

Developing a Board Policy that Incorporates the Planning Function into Board Responsibilities

One important way for the institution to incorporate planning into regular operations, is to develop and implement a board policy that supports the planning function. The policy sets the stage for commitment to the planning process and provides the board the opportunity to hold the administration accountable for functions identified in the plan.

Utilizing a Quarterly Reporting Process to Monitor Progress on Goals and Establish Accountability

The development and implementation of a quarterly reporting process is critical to ensuring that the mid-range plan is being utilized by each major division. Without a reporting mechanism in place, the institutional focus on planning is lost and goals are seldom achieved. An established system of accountability for key administrators, who must oversee the attainment of goals, is a vital part of the planning process. This reporting process also monitors progress toward goals, while identifying challenges that may be encountered thus providing a means to determine whether adjustments can be made that will facilitate goal achievement.

Implementation of a quarterly reporting mechanism provides a tool for key administrators to brief the president and the board on the status of goals in each division. Exhibit 6-1 provides an example of a quarterly report from the Finance and Operations Division.

EXHIBIT 6-1

MID-RANGE PLAN UPDATE
Pgs. 20-23 of the 2003-2007 Mid-Range Plan

Division: **Finance & Operations**
Reported by: **John Doe, Vice President of Finance &**
                     Operations
Period Ending: **June 30, 2003**

Goal #3, Pg. 23

Goal 3:   Provide the capital improvements, maintenance, equipment and additional resources for new and existing instructional programs and student services.

Goal 3a: Paint room 23
Comment: Change objective to read, "paint, carpet and replace furniture."

Goal 3b: Install exhaust system for Agriculture Power Tech Program.
Comment: Completed 9/2003.

Goal 3c: Refinish gym floor.
Comment: Completed 7/20/03.

Goal #5, pgs. 25, 26 and 27

Goal 5:   Provide technology to support campus operations.

Goal 5a,i : Test hardware/software for year 2000 compliance.
Comment: Completed 1/2000.

Goal 5a,ii: Upgrade 100 MB backbone between file and data servers.
Comment: Completed 3/2001.

Another benefit of utilizing a quarterly reporting process is that it improves communication between the president and the board. Deans and division administrators submit quarterly reports initially to the president for inclusion in board meeting materials. It is often beneficial for deans and division heads to present their reports in person to the board. The board agenda is built to allow time for members to present questions or concerns regarding the status of goals. It also allows the administration an opportunity and time to provide more detailed information regarding current challenges or issues that may be hindering progress. Incorporating quarterly reporting allows the board to utilize the planning process to effectively oversee institutional and divisional goal attainment.

Implementing an Annual Review of the Mid-Range Plan

The planning document, like the process that produced it, must be dynamic. The institution should realize growth, expansion and staff buy-in to the process as it continues each year. As progress is made toward attaining goals, the administration should identify needs to serve as a basis for new goals, delaying current goals, or eliminating goals in the plan that are no longer relevant. In order to reflect these changes and keep the mid-range plan current, it should be reviewed and updated annually.

The institution administrators should review the mid-range plan at three different points in the planning process. The first review should occur prior to the faculty and staff planning retreats so that administrators can obtain an overview of current goal status. This creates an opportunity for faculty and staff to review progress and provide input on goal relevancy, while developing new goals to be considered for the board planning session. The second review occurs immediately prior to the board planning session and during the development of the agenda. The administration reviews current division goals and the recommendations from the faculty and staff planning retreats. This provides a framework for briefing the board during the planning session on goal progress and recommended new goals. The third review is completed prior to the development of the revised plan. The person responsible for updating and revising the plan should draft, for key administrators, a new goal section for each division reflecting the outcomes of the faculty and staff planning retreats and board planning session. This review should result in identifying goals that have been completed, those that need to be delayed and goals that should be added. The revised plan should highlight goals that are completed, delayed and deleted. Such follow-up provides a means of tracking progress and ensuring a continuum in the planning process.

Incorporating notations into the revised plan provides a way to track goals throughout the planning process and to develop a history of goal attainment. Goals that have been completed should have the notation "complete" incorporated into the target date column. Completed goals are reflected in the updated plan for one year and then deleted thus serving as a historical record of achievement.

The administration may find that some goals, once having been achieved, are now part of the regular operations of the institution. A notation describing how often an activity is to occur should be provided in the plan. For example, a goal may have been established to develop a new recruiting process for nursing students. One of the objectives was to develop and implement a direct mail campaign to potential students. The goal has been completed, the recruiting process has been developed, and the nursing faculty has determined the objective — the direct mail campaign— needs to occur twice annually. The word "completed" will be noted in the goal's target date column. Beside the supporting objective, the word "biannually" would indicate it is now part of the regular operation of the nursing department and how frequently the activity occurs. In this example, the notations would be retained in the plan for one year to provide tracking.

Goals that were not attainable should remain in the plan with an extended target date. This indicates that the goal is still relevant, but because of decreased funding, lack of personnel resources, or other unforeseen challenges, the goal was not completed. It is also beneficial to provide a cross-reference to the previous year's plan to show when the initial goal was implemented and to indicate that it is being forwarded to the updated plan. The cross reference column would show the date of the mid-range plan, the page and goal number.

The administration may determine that it is necessary to delete some goals permanently, because of changes in institutional direction, unforeseen circumstances, or lack of relevancy. In this case, the goal is eliminated from the new version of the plan.

Exhibit 6-2 provides a sample goal page illustrating the use of notations to identify goal status. These notations are in bold type.

EXHIBIT 6-2

Mid-Range Plan, 2002-2007
Division: Student Services

Goals & Objectives	Target Date	Implementation/ Annual Costs	Acct.#	Office of Responsibility	Cross-Reference
Goal #1 — Increase student support services and course offerings to outlying communities and high schools in the service area, including use of alternative modes of delivery that are tailored to meet student demands and needs for course offerings.	May 2007	$10,000	11-1462 11-1463 11-1464	V.P., Student Services V.P. of Inst. Outreach Directors	**See 2001-2006 MRP, pg. 25, Goal #1.** **Goal carried forward.** **New target date established.**
a. Increase credit hour hour production to support institutional goal.	July 2004 **Completed Ongoing**				
i. Incorporate recruiting strategies established by the institution to ensure enrollment growth.	Sept. 2005 **Completed**	$25,000			
ii. Work to secure adequate enrollment in classes to prevent cancellation of courses and associated negative repercussions.	Aug. 2006	$ 5,500			
iii. Secure current software to offer competitive courses for business and industry.	May 2007 **Deleted — Moved to Business & Industry Program.**				

The processes described in this chapter close the planning loop. A completed planning calendar incorporating the processes discussed in this chapter has been provided in Exhibit 6-3. Processes described in this chapter have been italicized.

EXHIBIT 6-3

FINAL PLANNING CALENDAR

December — President sends directive to deans, directors and vice-presidents to begin the preparation necessary for the faculty, staff and board planning sessions.

January – *Key administrators review their respective sections of the mid-range plan and prepare a briefing for faculty and staff planning retreats.*
- Faculty and staff planning retreats conducted.
- *Quarterly reports are prepared by key administrators and submitted to the president for inclusion in board meeting materials.*

February – *Key administrators review their respective sections of the mid-range plan and prepare briefing for key administrative meetings scheduled prior to the board planning session.*
- Each dean, director and vice-president presents a briefing of revised goals and new goals to be presented to the board at a series of key administrative meetings.
- Planning guidelines and parameters are established.

March – Standing committee recommendations are submitted to the president and incorporated into the Board Planning Session agenda where appropriate.
- Capital projects priority list and budget submitted to president and incorporated in the board planning session agenda.
- Outcomes assessment goals to be incorporated into the mid-range plan are submitted to the president and incorporated into the board planning session agenda.

EXHIBIT 6-3 *(continued)*

- Program review recommendations are submitted to the chief academic officer and chief administrator of each functional area reviewed.
- *Key administrators review their respective sections of the mid-range plan in preparation for the board planning session.*
- Board planning session agenda finalized.

April – The board planning session is conducted.
- *Quarterly reports are incorporated into the presentation by key administrators at the board planning session.*

May – Division and departmental equipment plans are submitted.

June-July – Budget workshops are conducted and final budget prepared.
- Planning document prepared.
- *Quarterly report is prepared in July and submitted to the president for inclusion in board meeting materials.*
- *Key administrators prepare their updated sections of the mid-range plan.*

August – Planning document is presented to the board for approval.

September-February – Initiatives are underway to attain goals identified in the planning document.

Summary

The processes described in this chapter — establishing a board policy that addresses planning, utilizing quarterly reports, and developing an annual review of the mid-range plan —will lend stability to the planning process and ensure that it is continuous and viable for the institution. Other added benefits of using these processes include: 1) improving communication of the value and benefits of planning throughout the institution; 2) providing administrative accountability to ensure progress toward goal completion;

3) providing focus for the institution; and 4) attaining desired goals.

Conclusion

Today's high tech, high performance environment thrives on change, and planning is what makes for stability out of change. To plan is to deal with future uncertainty, in an informed manner, in order to minimize risk to the college. The one thing to remember is that the farther into the future an institution plans, the greater the risk as uncertainty grows. For this reason, business, industry, and many nonprofit organizations advocate mid-range planning over the traditional strategic planning models. What makes mid-range planning a more effective model for change is that it reduces the time horizon, and thus the unknown, into a manageable process. Setting goals for the next three to five years is based on environmental factors that are more accurate and predictable.

ENDORSEMENTS

During my tenure as chairman of the Association of Community College Trustees (ACCT), and in my present capacity on the Board of Directors of the American Association of Community Colleges (AACC), I have observed numerous instances of both outstanding progress and lack of progress among member colleges. In my opinion, what has made the difference is vision or lack of vision. The most progressive colleges have a clear vision of what they want to achieve, and a clearly defined pathway, i.e., a plan on how to reach that destination. A college without a plan is like a ship without a rudder, directionless without a clear destination in mind. As a long-time trustee, I know and have seen the value of planning. Whether at the national, state or local level, the value of a documented, well ordered set of goals and objectives keyed to the organization's mission cannot be overstated.

Community colleges are changing because of the demands they are faced with from business, industry and government. The federal government now recognizes the contribution and potential of community colleges; business and industry see our colleges as the primary provider of a skilled workforce; and "high tech" is part of our daily vocabulary. Many times these forces conflict, and at times they overlap. A well-though-out plan will go a long way toward avoiding the resulting confusion. Sound planning is being emphasized more to assure timely and effective responses to these demands, along with assuring the accomplishment of the goals and objectives that are shaping the 21st century role of our colleges. Planning processes have taken on a new importance, and planning is being tied more closely to accountability.

Because we must move swiftly and because the resulting future change is becoming more unpredictable, shorter term plans are replacing the 20-year strategic plans we experienced in the '80s and '90s of the last century. A mid-range planning process, i.e., three-five years is already becoming the norm. The mid-range planning process laid out in this book seems to fit the direction our colleges are going and the challenges they are facing. I have experienced its success both at that level and at my own commu-

95

nity college. Not only do I bring it to your attention, but I whole-heartedly endorse the process as being consistent with the demands of our times.

— Darrell Shumway
AACC, Board of Directors
2000 Chairman, ACCT

EDUKAN is an online consortium of six community colleges in western Kansas ... Dedra Manes (co-author of this process) consulted with the consortium to develop a strategic plan ... includes vision, mission and goals as well as steps necessary to achieve goals ... a complete package that allowed EDUKAN to respond appropriately to NCA (North Central Association).

— Gillian Gabelmann
Executive Director
EDUKAN

(Plan) was based on relevant and specific knowledge and experience in strategic planning (as used at) multiple community colleges. (Using this process) external and internal analysis of New Hampshire's economic and higher education needs was comprehensive ... identification of our system's strengths and weaknesses was accurate.

— Tom Wisbey
Deputy Commissioner
New Hampshire Technical
and Community College System